THE IMPACT OF SUPREME COURT DECISIONS

The Impact of Supreme Court
Decisions

EMPIRICAL STUDIES

EDITED BY

THEODORE L. BECKER
UNIVERSITY OF HAWAII

NEW YORK
OXFORD UNIVERSITY PRESS
LONDON   1969   TORONTO

To my reference group: Whose cohesion
each would resist,

But for whose interaction, this book
should not exist.

MARA, RAGS, TEMOANA, BIG TRAIN, DD,
PETUNIA, GRINGO, OTIS AND KAT.

Acknowledgments

This volume was conceived during a summer teaching stint at New York University and developed during the following fall, winter, and spring at Wayne State University in Detroit, Michigan. At the latter institution, several people became indispensable for the completion of this book. First, Norman Wengert and Tom Barnhart ran much needed administrative interference. For that I offer humble thanks. Second, Bob Mendelsohn was always a willing and able intellectual sounding board. Finally, all who have suffered through the tortures of cutting and pasting a reader together know that there is at least one noble, long-tried graduate assistant who really did the work. In this case, it was Steve Hendel. He was the buffer between me and insanity, at least for that year. Only time can tell whether I owe him a debt of gratitude for that.

T.L.B.

Honolulu, Hawaii
October 1968

Contents

"Does anybody know . . . where we can go to find light on what the practical consequences of these decisions have been?"

FELIX FRANKFURTER

This book is a collection of articles about the consequences of Supreme Court decisions. If the law expounded by the nine Justices had no effect on anyone, it would be only so many words in so many books. It is assumed, though, that the decisions of these judges are far reaching. It is assumed that they influence certain areas of social behavior, and for that reason they attract the attention of social scientists. It is assumed that they are capable of altering the behavior of political and governmental officials at all levels as well as the political behavior of the man on the street—which explains its allure for political scientists. Yet only in recent times has the investigation into the actual effects of the Supreme Court decision (in its generic sense) been pursued in earnest. A remarkable growth has taken place, witnessed by the appearance of innumerable research projects on the incredibly diverse effects of the decision. As is so often the case in life, interest is generating further interest.

I daresay that this new focus of research is the second important breakthrough in the modern study of the Supreme Court. The first began seriously some ten years ago when social scientific theories and methods first were put to use in trying to determine the relative importance of extra-legal factors on the judicial decision, in general, and the Supreme Court decision, in particular. However, this modern approach to the study of influences on the Supreme Court decision failed to spark much interest among other political scientists or in the community of legal scholars.

3

On the other hand, the modern empirical study of the impact of the Supreme Court decision promises to excite a resurgence of general interest in what the Justices are saying in the official opinions. This research, far more than that on the influences on the Supreme Court decision, directly merges the study of the Court into the study of politics. Extra-legal influence on the Court, though real and significant enough, ordinarily is indirect and subtle and essential data are very difficult to obtain. The picture of the Court's impact, though, is far easier to draw and makes a far more inviting canvas. As far as impact is concerned, the relationships, like American politics in the raw, are intricate, multi-leveled, and multi-dimensional. Indeed, the pertinent findings in this area of research should have appeal for nearly every student of American politics. Those interested in the influences on the Supreme Court decision were concerned principally with legal processes; those interested in the impact of the Supreme Court decision are concerned more about political and social change. This is not to deny importance to the work on the psychological, sociological, and political influence on Supreme Court decision-making; it is to place it in proper perspective.

I have decided to arrange the essays comprising this anthology according to the various political locales where the impact is felt (Congress, federal administrative agencies, local police departments, etc.). Of course, the way a man cuts and distributes a pie can reveal his values. So it is with the slicing of a book into parts, chapters, and sections. Such categories are a fair indicator of the theoretical bias of an author or editor. Should he be a devious sort of a fellow, and should the time be ripe, classification can be a sly way to push a pet theory without making his intentions clear. It so happens that theory-pushing is not my objective, although the amount of research on the consequences of the Supreme Court decision has ballooned to such proportions that it almost requires theoretical guidance to point the way.

In all candor, though, the seeds of a theory are probably inherent in the subsequent compartmentalization of materials. The division according to where impact takes place in the political system manifests my own hunch that this is an important, if not the most directly intervening, element to be taken into account in the development of a theory on the effects of the Supreme Court decision.[1] However, the main reason for the division of this book as it is so divided is simpler and more mundane: The research itself infrequently cuts across the location of impact. Most research articles concern themselves exclusively or mainly with one arena of government. Presently it would be difficult to classify the available research by any other variable, for example, by the degree of compliance or by types of evasion or defiance. For that matter, it would also be difficult to classify the literature according to what the researchers believe are the chief extra-governmental conditioning factors (e.g., attitudes, social background of the decision-makers, degree of urbanization of a community) that account for the variations in impact of the Supreme Court decision. Partly out of editorial inclination and partly out of necessity, then, the sections of this volume are the effect of the Court's decisions on (1) Congress and the President; (2) the lower courts; (3) local and state government and politics; and (4) public opinion.

To introduce these studies, I have chosen an article that is cited by nearly every modern researcher who chooses to trade in the results of Supreme Court decisions. Indeed, the current splurge of political science research on the Court's impact echoes this eloquent plea written several years ago by Professor Arthur S. Miller.[2] As the reader will see, Miller is concerned with how social scientific research can serve the vital interests of the Supreme Court itself. In this day and age his worry over this matter might best be shared by us all; and that includes the Justices too. After all, the Court's impact on America has contributed to the first Congressional repudiation in well over a century of a nominee for the post of Chief Justice. The

1. Donald Reich believes that the best way of organizing research on judicial impact is by specifying the possible relationships that the Court enters into through its decision-making. Many of these relationships are organized by the framework of government; thus, his scheme is highly related to the structure of government, as is the one in this volume. See his "The Impact of Supreme Court Decision-Making," unpublished paper (Oberlin College).

2. Two other recent calls and suggestions for further research in this area are: Ernest M. Jones, "Impact Research and Sociology of Law: Some Tentative Proposals," *Wisconsin Law Review* (Spring, 1966), pp. 1–9; Richard Lempert, "Strategies of Research Design in the Legal Impact Study," *Law and Society Review* 1 (November, 1966), pp. 111–32.

Court's impact also became, in 1968, one of the key planks in the platform of one of the strongest third-party Presidential challenges in America's history. In 1968 the Court also saw some of its important decisions of recent years effectively reversed by Congressional action. Obviously, the need for knowledge about the impact of Supreme Court decisions is greater than ever.

ARTHUR SELWYN MILLER

On the Need for "Impact Analysis" of Supreme Court Decisions

* * *

THE ELEMENTS OF IMPACT ANALYSIS

Understanding of the Supreme Court and of its role in the American system will be furthered by systematic and comprehensive attention paid to the social impact of Court decisions. Impact analysis has at least two facets: (a) an appreciation by judges of the consequences of their decisions; and (b) an evaluation by commentators of the social effect of judicial decisions. It looks to the consequences of judicial decisions and evaluates them in accordance with the extent to which they further the attainment of societal goals. It thus involves asking what the law should be as well as what it is. "[D]emocracy," Frank H. Knight has said, "has assumed the task, enormously more difficult than enforcing a law known to all, of deciding what the law ought to be and making any changes called for." [1] That statement pinpoints the problem in constitutional adjudication: the need for deciding what the law "ought to be."

Now, what constitutional law "ought to be" in substantive terms is a question beyond the scope of this article. It is, nonetheless, meet to say that we should not forget, as indeed lawyers have often forgotten, that the Constitution (and the social order it governs) was

1. Knight, *On the Meaning of Justice*, in NOMOS VI: JUSTICE 1, 2 (Friedrich & Chapman eds. 1963).

From the *Georgetown Law Journal*, 53: 2 (1965), pp. 365–401. Reprinted by permission of the publisher and the author.

Arthur S. Miller is Professor of Law at the George Washington University Law School.

established for certain, quite definite purposes. Without going into the question of what may have been the "real" motivations of the fifty-five men now revered in America's hagiology as the Founding Fathers, the Preamble to the Constitution itself sets forth the objects for which it was written: "to form a more perfect union, establish justice, insure domestic tranquility, provide for the common defense, promote the general welfare, and secure the blessings of liberty. . . ." These familar words set the tone, and Mr. Chief Justice John Marshall's opinion in *McCulloch* [2] thirty-two years later established the method—by adding the concept of an evolving Constitution—through which American constitutional development has taken place. Constitutional interpretation has proceeded side by side with legislation (and, in the present century, with administrative law-making) to make up a legal system by which the ideals set forth in the Preamble have been and are being furthered.

An essential point here is *change,* which is a primary characteristic of American society (for a number of reasons, not least of which is the scientific-technological revolution) and which may be seen throughout American law, both public and private. Constitutional change, it is submitted, should be evaluated in terms of whether or not it tends to further the ideals of the Preamble. As Knight has said: "The real task faced is that of social progress, definable only as a *direction* of change (in a complex sense, mostly negative) through alleviating some of the grosser *in*justices that a society can agree upon and find remediable." [3] The accomplishment of that task can be helped through impact analysis, for it is only when given decisions are criticized and evaluated in terms of postulated goals that it can be determined whether social progress is being attained, just as initially it is only through attention to consequences that the Court can determine the criteria for particular decisions. Impact analysis cannot set the goals of decision-making—that has to come from elsewhere—but can assist in two ways: (a) in providing a basis for decision and (b) in evaluating the decisions themselves.

*   *   *

2. McCulloch v. Maryland, 17 U.S. (4 Wheat.) 316 (1819).
3. Knight, *supra* note 1, at 3.

. . . Thousands of words have been written, for example, about the recent voting cases and about the school prayer decisions. But those who approve and those who decry have one common ground: they do not provide readers with any basis for explaining why they accept one premise over another. It is here that "impact analysis" would seem to be of some assistance. The following hypothesis is suggested as a way of thinking about the problem: *Choices are made by Justices from among conflicting principles (or inconsistent interests) not because of compelling law, but because of an evaluation of what the impact of given decisions is thought to be.*[4] As said above, the judicial decision is a law-creating institution; in it, the Justices seek to manage a segment of the future. Rather than engaging solely in retrospection, the Justices are also looking forward—result-oriented, in the noninvidious sense of the term—as much as they are concept-oriented.

Holmes, as usual, noted the situation many years ago when he stated:

> I think that the judges themselves have failed adequately to recognize their duty of weighing considerations of social advantage. The duty is inevitable, and the result of the often proclaimed judicial aversion to deal with such considerations is simply to leave the very ground and foundation of judgments inarticulate, and often unconscious, as I have said.
>
> . . . I cannot but believe that if the training of lawyers led them habitually to consider more definitely and explicitly the social advantage on which the rule they lay down must be justified, they sometimes would hesitate where now they are confident, and see that really they were taking sides upon debatable and burning questions.[5]

The Holmesian statement still holds true, at least in part. But it can be extended somewhat: it is submitted that judges normally do weigh "considerations of social advantage"—i.e., take the consequences of their decisions into account—whether or not they articulate those considerations in their opinions. As Holmes said, this is "inevitable" and unavoidable. The question is not: Should a judge take policy

4. *Cf.* WASSERSTROM, THE JUDICIAL DECISION 172–73 (1961). . . .
5. Holmes, *The Path of the Law*, 10 HARV. L. REV. 457, 467–68 (1897).

considerations into account? Rather it is this: Which policy should he choose? For choose he must, however his opinion may be phrased.

It is in private law as well as public law that a jurisprudence of consequences may be discerned. And it is, as I have said, familiar learning. But it needs repeating because it has not struck home and has not become widely accepted by lawyers generally. The essential point is that the Supreme Court in constitutional adjudications, hearing as it does only a handful of cases each year, deals with a fluid situation, and, accordingly, must look forward as well as back. It must "legislate," at least in part, and determine what the law should be as well as what it is. This is because each case that comes before it, and is decided on the merits, is in basic part unique.

But saying that the Court does "legislate" via impact analysis does not necessarily mean that it should openly avow that it does. Nor does it answer the questions of how much "legislation" and when.

The Need for Expertise

A jurisprudence of consequences poses complex problems. In the first place, impact analysis makes the task of adjudication enormously more complicated. For judges to weigh considerations of social advantage is a far more difficult job than to apply rules or principles in given cases. If done in any systematic and thoroughgoing manner, it calls for a quality of expertise on the part of both judges and lawyers for which their legal education will not have prepared them. As Cardozo said forty years ago:

> Some of the errors of courts have their origin in imperfect knowledge of the economic and social consequences of a decision, or of the economic and social needs to which a decision will respond. In the complexities of modern life there is a constantly increasing need for resort by the judges to some fact-finding agency which will substitute exact knowledge of factual conditions for conjecture and impression.[6]

Reference to one situation may serve to indicate the problem more specifically: antitrust law. The Sherman Act has all the attributes of a constitutional provision. Both in the original statute, which is

6. CARDOZO, THE GROWTH OF THE LAW (1924), at 116–17.

couched in generalized terms, and in its exegesis by the Court there may be seen a close analogy to "pure" constitutional cases. Writing a decade ago, Mr. Justice Frankfurter made the following statement concerning the judicial task in antitrust cases:

> Take a problem that has been confronting the Supreme Court, Sherman Law regulation of the movie industry. A number of decisions have been rendered finding violations under the Sherman Law. Does anybody know, when we have a case, as we had one the other day, where we can go to find light on what the practical consequences of these decisions have been? . . . I don't know to what extent these things can be ascertained. I do know that, to the extent that they may be relevant in deciding cases, they ought not to be left to the blind guessing of myself and others only a little less uninformed than I am.[7]

What bothered Mr. Justice Frankfurter should trouble his colleagues on the bench, as well as all other members of the legal profession. The decisions of the Supreme Court in Sherman Act cases, since, as John R. Commons said, it acts as "the first authoritative faculty of political economy in the world,"[8] have important consequences for the nature of the American economy and for the government-business relationship. Should the Supreme Court act as blindly as Frankfurter suggests it does? Should it not have greater assistance from members of the bar, plus aid from political economists in making the essentially economic decisions involved in antitrust law? Such a suggestion has in fact been proffered by lawyer-economist Mark S. Massel of The Brookings Institution. In a paper published in 1962, Massel concluded:

> It seems clear that means must be found to alleviate the burden of the judges in order to insure significant application of the public intent behind the antitrust laws. . . . Obviously, such efforts should not be based on any belief that they would reduce the importance of judicial judgment. . . . Economic advice can be used to help to define the issues, to organize data, to suggest analysis of evidence and precedent, to outline available alternatives for the

7. FRANKFURTER, SOME OBSERVATIONS ON SUPREME COURT LITIGATION AND LEGAL EDUCATION 17 (1954).
8. COMMONS, LEGAL FOUNDATIONS OF CAPITALISM 7 (1924).

judicial decision, and to make reasonable predictions about the consequences of such alternatives.[9]

This calls for a level of expertise not often found within the legal profession, on or off the bench, for lawyers must be able to utilize the insights of economists. It is, furthermore, questionable at the present time whether the skills of economists measure up to the need set forth by Massel. But is there any feasible alternative to following up on his suggestion, once one accepts the Frankfurter proposition that the Justices on the Court are milling around in the dark without effective guidance?

*   *   *

But if judges are not experts in economics, they also are not particularly expert in many other areas of societal concern in which their decisions have an impact. Can the same argument be made for judicial abdication in such areas as the position of ethnic groups (principally, the Negroes) in this country, the administration of criminal law, the separation of church and state, and representation in legislatures? All of these decisional areas have found the Supreme Court under attack from one source or another.

*   *   *

. . . Furthermore, how are the Justices to determine the validity of the learning from such disciplines as economics, political science and sociology?[10] Is there such agreement among the practitioners of these esoteric pursuits that a lawyer may without fear accept the statements of any of them? The answer to that, quite obviously, is no. Accordingly, there is the further problem of evaluating the conflicting propositions advanced by equally respected members of the non-

9. Massel, *Economic Analysis in Judicial Antitrust Decisions*, 20 A.B.A. ANTI-TRUST SECTION 46, 58 (1962). *Compare* Friendly, *Reactions of Lawyer—Newly Become Judge*, 71 YALE L.J. 218, 221-27 (1961), *with* Hyneman, *Free Speech: At What Price?*, 56 AM. POL. SCI. REV. 847 (1962). Hyneman states: "[N]one of the judges to date . . . has so far produced an opinion that stands as proof that his decision rests on a comprehensive, sharply discriminating and systematic scrutiny of the known and probable social consequences of the act under consideration." *Id.* at 851.

10. See Frank, *The Lawyer's Role in Modern Society*, 4 J. PUB. L. 8 (1955).

legal professions. The flow of information to the Court, according to the orthodox notion, is via the briefs and argument of counsel, the record of the trial court and the concept of judicial notice. This must be augmented, either through the invention of new techniques or by improving present methods, if that flow is to provide the Justices with the valid insights of disciplines other than law. It will do little good, and perhaps much harm, if all that is furnished is the competing "wisdom" of experts for both sides of the case, experts who may be expected to testify in accordance with the desires of the party retaining them. The "fallacy of the impartial expert" should be recognized, if not exploded. The problem that this poses is of major proportions: the Justices can and do take the consequences of their decisions into account; should they continue to operate on the basis of assumptions and untested hypotheses? If not, then how is the situation to be improved? [11]

* * *

THE PERSPECTIVE OF THE "DISINTERESTED" OBSERVER

The main task of the commentator upon the Supreme Court and its jurisprudence is to contribute to the understanding of that peculiar American institution. An important secondary task is to provide a flow of informed commentary which will serve the purpose of constructive criticism of the Court and its work, and thus assist in keeping the Justices within proper bounds. These are no mean jobs. On the contrary, they call for a combination of insight and judgment which requires meticulous attention to detail as well as a grasp of the theory and philosophy of judicial action. Moreover, the products of this effort have a definite, albeit unmeasurable, impact upon the decisional process. Commentators upon the Supreme Court form a part of the law-making process of the Court.[12] Constitutional law is

11. Judge Charles Wyzanski met this problem by appointing an economist as one of his "law" clerks when he had an important case before him. See KAYSEN, UNITED STATES v. UNITED SHOE MACHINERY CORPORATION: AN ECONOMIC ANALYSIS OF AN ANTITRUST CASE (1956).

12. Compare Newland, Press Coverage of the United States Supreme Court, 17 WESTERN POLITICAL Q. 15 (1964), with Newland, The Supreme Court and Legal Writing: Learned Journals as Vehicles of an Anti-antitrust Lobby?, 48 GEO. L.J. 105 (1959).

not a completed, but a growing and self-correcting, system. It grows by what Morris Raphael Cohen called "the interaction between social usage and the work of legislatures, courts, and administrative officials, and even legal text writers." [13] The growing incidence of law review material cited in Supreme Court opinions is testimony of the extent to which legal writers have influence upon the Justices [14] (or, at the very least, of the extent to which Justices consider such writings helpful in buttressing their previously made decisions).

Contribution to the understanding of the Supreme Court and its product will come about when the commentators develop valid descriptive or predictive rules *about* constitutional law and its creation and operation as distinguished from rules *of* constitutional law. As Cohen put it, we should not forget that

> law is essentially concerned with norms that regulate, rather than with uniformities that describe, human conduct. The laws that natural science seeks to discover . . . are uniformities which if valid at all cannot be violated. . . . But it is of the very essence of legal rules that they are violable and that penalties or sanctions are provided for their various violations. They do not state what always is, but attempt to decide what ought to be.[15]

The difference is between the "scientific validity of real rules *about* law . . . [and] the legal validity of rules *of* law . . . ." [16] Impact analysis permits insight to be attained into the operative rules *about* law, the rules of how law acts in the social milieu.[17]

Constitutional law degenerates into theology and barren exegeses upon the sacred text of the Constitution unless and until it is tested by its consequences. But for such testing to be accomplished attention must be accorded at least three matters, each of which has re-

13. M. R. Cohen, Reason and Law 76 (1950).
14. Reynolds v. Sims, 377 U.S. 533 (1964), is particularly noteworthy in this respect.
15. M. R. Cohen, Law and the Social Order 205 (1933).
16. Rumble, *American Legal Realism and the Reduction of Uncertainty*, 13 J. Pub. L. 45, 75 (1964).
17. See McDougal, *The Ethics of Applying Systems of Authority: The Balanced Opposites of a Legal System*, in The Ethics of Powers: The Interplay of Religion, Philosophy, and Politics 231 (Laswell & Cleveland eds. 1962).

ceived little attention in scholarly commentary upon the Supreme Court: (a) an appreciation of the ends sought to be served by the process called constitutional law (and, accordingly, of the ends of American society itself); (b) a method of ascertaining the causal connection between judicial decision and social change, by no means a self-evident proposition; and (c) knowledge of what may broadly be called the political economy of American constitutionalism (the political science, the economics, the psychology, the sociology).

Merely listing these indicates the poverty of knowledge about the constitutional adjudicative process that is the unhappy present fact. Not only do most commentators fail to take the ends or purposes of law and society into account, some even go so far as to deny vehemently that it is a proper inquiry. The most that can be said for that point-of-view is that it tends to relegate discussion of the Supreme Court and its jurisprudence to the same sort of sterile exercises that characterized theological literature during the Middle Ages: endless discussion about minute doctrinal points. To be sure, there is some value in doctrinal clarification. To quote Cohen again:

> [W]ithout the use of concepts and general principles we can have no science, or intelligible systematic account, of the law or of any other field. And the demand for system in the law is urgent not only on theoretical but also on practical grounds. Without general ideas, human experience is dumb as well as blind.[18]

The point, however, is that more is needed than concepts and general principles. That "more" is the three matters listed above: the ends of law, the causal connection, the political economy of American constitutionalism.

Just as there is an absence of systematic attention paid to the ends of law, so too is there a paucity of knowledge about the relationship between judicial decision and social change. Many observers make statements of an a priori nature. Others proceed on assumptions, acting as if there were causal connections between Court decisions and social change without examination of the bases of those assumptions. Typical are those who have been called "police-prosecution oriented critics of the Courts"—those who assert that judicial deci-

18. M. R. COHEN, *op. cit. supra* note 13, at 63.

sions have had the consequence of antisocial behavior. Professor
Yale Kamisar in a recent article has effectively shown the untenable
factual foundation of such criticism.[19]

*   *   *

. . . The gap may be seen with particular clarity in the plethora
of law journal articles which have been produced discussing *Baker v.
Carr*[20] and its aftermath. In this commentary there is an almost
complete lack of reference to the manner in which the political
system of this nation operates.[21] Some critics line up on one side, in
full bay in their denunciation of the decisions; while on the other
side, the defenders stand in measured array, stoutly affirming the
Court in the apportionment cases.[22] For both sides it may be said that
they have made little factual inquiry whatever as to the meaning for
the political structure of the cases.[23]

*   *   *

19. Kamisar, *On the Tactics of Police-Prosecution Oriented Critics of the
Court*, 49 CORNELL L.Q. 436 (1964).
20. 369 U.S. 186 (1962).
21. See, *e.g.*, Friedelbaum, *Baker v. Carr: The New Doctrine of Judicial Intervention and Its Implications for American Federalism*, 29 U. CHI. L. REV. 673
(1962); Lucas, *Legislative Apportionment and Representative Government:
The Meaning of Baker v. Carr*, 61 MICH. L. REV. 711 (1963); McCloskey,
Foreword: The Reapportionment Case, 76 HARV. L. REV. 54 (1962); McKay,
Political Thickets and Crazy Quilts: Reapportionment and Equal Protection,
61 MICH. L. REV. 645 (1963). . . .
22. The commentators upon the reapportionment decisions seem to proceed by
what Holmes once called the "inspirational" method. "I sometimes tell students," Holmes said in 1899, "that the law schools pursue an inspirational
combined with a logical method, that is, the postulates are taken for granted
upon authority without inquiry into their worth, and then logic is used as the
only tool to develop the results." Holmes, *Law in Science and Science in Law*,
in COLLECTED LEGAL PAPERS 210, 238 (1920). But the question in the reapportionment decisions is not so much the logic as the worth of the postulates
from which both the Justices and the commentators proceed.
23. *But see* Goldberg, *The Statistics of Malapportionment*, 72 YALE L.J. 90
(1962).

1 The Effect on the President and Congress

The Supreme Court is one of three constitutionally co-equal branches of the federal government. Still it was only owing to the political guile of Chief Justice John Marshall in 1803 that the Court managed to get and keep the vital power to declare acts of the President and laws of Congress unconstitutional. The vehicle for this judicial *coup* was the famous case of *Marbury v. Madison*. Since then, the ensuing political equilibrium that constitutes our legal "check and balance system" has been a delicate one, and it has been disturbed seriously and often throughout the years.

The long history of friction between the Court and the President endured well into the twentieth century.[1] It has been dramatized by classic quotations and by tragicomic proposals. One statement that has weathered the years is tough, old Andrew Jackson's "John Marshall has made his decision, now let him enforce it." One of the more prominent suggestions for changing the Court's very fiber was FDR's abortive court-packing proposal of the late nineteen-thirties. Curiously, though, this struggle may have run its course. In 1952, during the Korean War emergency, President Truman swiftly and meekly acquiesced to the Court's invalidating his confiscation of the steel mill industry. Since then there has not been even the faintest hint of a skirmish between the Court and the three succeeding Presidents—even when sizable portions of the American population

1. See Glendon Schubert, *The Presidency in the Courts* (Minneapolis: University of Minnesota Press, 1957).

have been outraged by some Court decision or decisions. We may be entering an era of unprecedented good will between these two centers of political power.

Congress, on the other hand, remains as irascible as ever. It has exhibited profound reactions throughout history, continues to do so today, and promises to do much the same tomorrow. This is probably the reason why it still draws the undivided attention of many political scientists interested in studying the Court's effect: There is abundant sound and fury, and it signifies *something*.

Congress receives the impact of a Supreme Court decision directly and indirectly. The direct effect of a decision is experienced when the Court rebuffs a federal statute as being unconstitutional or construes a statute so far beyond what Congress wanted that it becomes apparent the Court felt the measure to be unwise or unreasonable. The indirect effect is experienced subsequent to a direct consequence on some state constituency; that is, when a state or local action has been declared unconstitutional. The Congressman himself may be offended (being "just plain homefolks" too); there may be widespread local indignation; some powerful interests might be hurt, and they are not loath or slow to convey their anguish to The Hill.

When a Supreme Court decision irks Congress directly or indirectly, Congress has ample power to retaliate. The weaponry it can field against the Court is impressive. Among the heavier artillery, Congress can initiate the constitutional amending process to undo a Court decision or to curtail the Court's power. In the medium range, it can redo a law that the Court has knocked down, or pare Court jurisdiction by statute. Sometimes the retribution could be classified as harassment or terrorism. For instance, Congress can direct darts and arrows at the place where it stings the most: The Pocketbook. Witness, for example, the House of Representatives frustrating a proposed pay increase for the Justices in 1965. As the reader plainly can see, Congress can really play it tough and rough. As the reader will see, it does.

Two of the leading modern books on this paradoxically hostile-dependent relationship between the Court and Congress were published about one year apart. One is *Congress Versus the Supreme Court* by C. Herman Pritchett; the other is Walter Murphy's *Con-*

gress and the Court.[2] Each deals with the historical parameters of the conflict but each focuses on the vigorous Congressional opposition to a series of specific decisions made in the 1956–57 term. In this instance, the cases had a strong pro-civil liberties bias and many local reactions were intensely negative; a concerted conservative counterattack was mounted locally—from sea to shining sea. Furthermore, many of these decisions were made within a very short period of time of each other, which helped foster a perception by those opposed to them that the cases were intended by the justices to be a sharp and brazen rebuke. The reply to such impunity had to be both sustained and bitter; Congress got the message and acted accordingly. Despite the consequent severity of the Congressional response, Pritchett and Murphy both believe that at that time the bark was much worse than the bite. Nevertheless, although no definitive action was taken against the Court, the Court apparently felt vulnerable enough to modify its position in subsequent cases. In other words, the Court withdrew unceremoniously from its newly gained outpost. Perhaps this was unnecessary, perhaps it was prudent. It is still too early to tell.

The three essays in this section employ a wide assortment of modern political science approaches to investigate a wide variety of interactions between the Court and Congress. The William Beaney —Edward Beiser article, for instance, employs a political-process/ case-study approach to analyze the effect of Congressional hearings on legislation proposed to limit Court jurisdiction. Their essay contains much information on the sources of the Court's political strength in the face of a frontal assault on its institutional power. Stuart Nagel's article systematically classifies and analyzes extensive historical data in order to find out what factors might be necessary for Congressional effectiveness in curbing the Court by legislation. Finally, Harry Stumpf deduces some specific hypotheses from more general materials and, through the use of some statistics, tries to see whether the use of the Court as a symbol in Congressional debate has any effect in obstructing anti-Court legislation.

2. C. Herman Pritchett, *Congress Versus the Supreme Court* (Minneapolis: University of Minnesota Press, 1961); Walter Murphy, *Congress and the Court* (Chicago: University of Chicago Press, 1962).

WILLIAM M. BEANEY
EDWARD N. BEISER

Prayer and Politics: The Impact of Engel and Schempp on the Political Process

* * *

. . . [I]t seems obvious that students of our legal system should not be satisfied with an acceptance of the official theory that court decisions, and particularly Supreme Court decisions that affect important public policy issues, are universally accepted as the law. It is grossly misleading and dangerous to treat law as a significant form of social control by concentrating on the rules handed down by courts. The realist persuasion in legal philosophy, if it has done nothing else, has warned us against ignoring the ways in which law affects or may leave untouched the daily lives of those to whom it ostensibly applies.

When a court decision impinges on an activity of only a few persons, the tracing of impact is a simple and obvious process. A *Steel Seizure* case,[1] for example, poses a single question with respect to consequences: Did the United States relinquish control of the seized mills to their private corporate owners? But seldom will the question and the answer be so simple. Some decisions, such as those affecting the right of free speech of a curbstone orator, may have few consequences beyond resolving the specific dispute because of the varying contexts in which official action curtailing speech takes place. The impact of decisions affecting behavior of law en-

1. Youngstown Sheet & Tube Co. v. Sawyer, 343 U.S. 579 (1952).

From *Journal of Public Law,* 13: 2 (1964), pp. 475–503. Reprinted by permission of the publisher and the authors.

William M. Beaney is a Professor of Politics at Princeton University. Edward N. Beiser is a Lecturer in Political Science at Williams College.

forcement officials are difficult to trace because of the difficulty of observing post-decision conduct. If any conclusions are to be reached they must inevitably be based on the judgment of a few well-placed observers, or on the frequency of future cases where a breach of the rule of the earlier decision can be documented.

These preliminary remarks are intended to serve as qualifications of the present brief study of some of the principal political and governmental responses to *Engel v. Vitale*,[2] in June 1962, outlawing the use of a Regent's prescribed prayer in New York public schools, and the decision of *School Dist. v. Schempp* [3]–*Murray v. Curlett* [4] in June 1963, prohibiting the reading of Bible passages or saying of prayers as religious exercises in public schools throughout the nation . . . A careful state-by-state study of what has occurred since these Court pronouncements has not been undertaken because of limitations of time and resources. What follows is based on data available in newspaper and other printed accounts, supplemented by interviews with those possessing first-hand knowledge of various facets of this subject.

THE NEW YORK PRAYER CASE

The reaction to the Court's decision declaring unconstitutional the use in public schools of a prayer prepared by the New York Regents was not long in forthcoming. And, at least in Congress, it was as one-sided as it was violent. Senator Talmadge (D. Ga.) denounced the decision as "unconscionable . . . an outrageous edict. . . ." [5] Congressman Williams (D. Miss.) insisted that the decision constituted "a deliberately and carefully planned conspiracy to substitute materialism for spiritual values and thus to communize America." [6] Congressman Sikes' (D. Fla.) description of the Court's action as infamous was probably closer to the mood of Congress than Senator Sparkman's (D. Ala.) milder comment: "a tragic mistake." [7] And

2. 370 U.S. 421 (1962).
3. 374 U.S. 203 (1963).
4. *Ibid.*
5. 108 CONG. REC. 11675 (1962).
6. *Id.* at 11734.
7. *Id.* at 11775, 11844.

Congressman Becker (R. N.Y.), who was to become the leader of the opposition to the Court on this issue, informed his colleagues that *Engel* was "the most tragic decision in the history of the United States." [8]

The immediate congressional reaction stressed what was to become one of the major themes of opponents of the Court's decisions: any opposition to religious activities in the public schools was an attack upon religion and upon God Himself. For Senator Robertson (D. Va.) this was the most extreme ruling the Supreme Court had ever made in favor of atheists and agnostics.[9] And Congressman Abernathy (D. Miss.) insisted that it would be "most pleasing to a few atheists and world Communism." [10] . . .

* * *

Congressional reaction was expressed in several other forms as well. Congressman Haley (D. Fla.) offered an amendment to a judiciary appropriations bill to earmark out of the Supreme Court's appropriations funds to purchase "for the personal use of each justice a copy of the Holy Bible," but his resolution was rejected 47-66.[11] And on September 27, the House voted unanimously to place the motto "In God We Trust" behind the Speaker's desk. Lest the motivation behind this sudden religious impulse escape anyone, Congressman Randall (D. Mo.) pointed out that "we have given perhaps not directly but yet in a not so subtle way" our answer to the Supreme Court's decision.[12]

The type of Congressional action which posed the most serious threat to the Court's holding, and with which this article will be primarily concerned, was the introduction of proposed amendments to the Constitution to allow public schools to conduct religious exercises. Congressman Frank Becker (R. N.Y.) introduced his amendment the day after *Engel* was decided. His language is typical of this

8. *Id.* at 11719.
9. *Id.* at 11708.
10. *Id.* at 11718.
11. 108 CONG. REC. 14360 (1962).
12. *Id.* at 21102.

type of proposal: "Prayers may be offered in the course of any program in any public school or other public place in the United States." [13]

Twenty-two senators and fifty-three representatives introduced amendments in response to *Engel*, as indicated in the following table: [14]

Table 1

MEMBERS OF CONGRESS INTRODUCING ANTI-*Engel* AMENDMENTS.
87TH CONGRESS, 2D SESSION.

Party Affiliation	House	Senate
Republicans	26	12
Southern Democrats	19	8
Non-Southern Democrats	8	2
Total	53	22

Congressional hostility toward the Court's decision was further demonstrated at hearings conducted by Senator Eastland's Judiciary Committee, just one month after *Engel* was decided. Testimony by various senators shows that they were acutely aware that the Court was soon to consider the constitutionality of Bible reading and the recitation of the Lord's Prayer in public schools, and that it was fully expected that both practices would be prohibited. Thus one of the joint resolutions before the committee anticipated the Court's action in *Schempp*, by proposing to amend the Constitution to allow prayer and Bible reading in public schools. It is interesting to note that in their general frame of reference as well as in their specific resolutions, the senators were significantly affected not only by what the Court had done—but by what it might be expected to do in the future.

*   *   *

13. Quoted in *Hearings on Prayer in Public Schools and Other Matters Before the Senate Committee on the Judiciary*, 87th Cong., 2d Sess. 71 (1962) [hereinafter cited as 1962 *Senate Hearings*].
14. "Southern Democrats" includes representatives of the eleven states of the old Confederate States of America. This is the usage of V. O. Key in SOUTHERN POLITICS (1949).

The short Senate Judiciary Committee hearings, with Senator Eastland, the chairman, absent, provided a field day for opponents of the Court. While the critical statements of such organizations as the American Legion and Young Americans For Freedom were countered by statements submitted by such groups as the American Civil Liberties Union, Anti-Defamation League, The Baptist Joint Committee on Public Affairs, and others, the oral testimony of the witnesses was unanimous in opposing the Court's action. The principal theme of the several witnesses—as had been the case in the initial congressional reaction—was that the decision represented a concerted attack on God and on religion in American life. Bishop Pike, for example, insisted that the result of the decision was "secularism, whether by intent or by default. I am not implying for a moment that the proponents or supporters of the decision of the Supreme Court intentionally wish an atheistic result. Nevertheless, when it is by default we simply *cut off the whole spiritual dimension of life,* and without even a reference to it. What we have left is actually a secularist view of life." [15]

The Eastland Committee hearings also provided a platform for those who had other bones to pick with the Court. There were repeated references in the testimony to persistent abuses by the Supreme Court of its judicial function. It is hardly coincidental that the overwhelming majority of congressmen and senators who participated in these hearings were Southerners. Table 1 indicated that more than half of the amendments to the Constitution introduced to reverse *Engel* were introduced by representatives of the 11 states of the former Confederacy. And Bishop Pike—the one non-congressional witness at the hearings—began his testimony with a strong states' rights argument.[16] Apart from allowing opponents of the Court and of the *Regents' Prayer* decision to vent their spleen, the hearings accomplished nothing. No final report was issued, nor was any legislation proposed.

15. *1962 Senate Hearings* 56. (Emphasis added.)
16. *Id.* at 51. Bishop Pike misstated the text of the 10th amendment in his comment that the amendment "makes clear that those things not *specifically* given to the federal government by authority, are reserved to the States and the people." (Emphasis added.)

The reaction of the late President Kennedy differed significantly. In response to a question at his regular news conference, he said:

> The Supreme Court has made its judgment. Some will disagree and others will agree. In the efforts we're making to maintain our Constitutional principles, we will have to abide by what the Supreme Court says. We have a very easy remedy here, and that is to pray ourselves. We can pray a good deal more at home and attend our churches with fidelity and emphasize the true meaning of prayer in the lives of our children. I hope, as a result of that decision, all Americans will give prayer a greater emphasis.[17]

The late President Hoover, however, voiced a strong dissent:

> The interpretation of the Constitution is a disintegration of one of the most sacred of American heritages. The Congress should at once submit an amendment to the Constitution which establishes the right to religious devotion in all government agencies—national, state, or local.[18]

* * *

THE RESPONSE TO THE LORD'S PRAYER AND BIBLE READING DECISIONS [19]

When the decision in *Schempp* was handed down on June 17, 1963, the immediate reaction was less violent than those who had experienced the stormy reaction to *Engel* had anticipated. . . .

* * *

. . . In any event, the generally milder initial reaction to the 1963 decision was to prove illusory to those who thought that this portended widespread acceptance of the Court's ruling. Both in the affected states and in Congress, unmistakable evidence of resistance and opposition in various forms soon appeared and battle was joined.

* * *

17. *CLSA Bull.* 3.
18. *Ibid.*
19. School Dist. v. Schempp, 374 U.S. 203 (1963).

THE BECKER AMENDMENT

In light of popular support for the continuation of Bible reading and prayers in the public schools, and the obvious reluctance of many states to abandon practices which have been in effect for several decades, it was hardly to be expected that Congress would stay out of the controversy engendered by the 1963 decision. The initial congressional reaction, though largely reflecting opposition, was more restrained than that of a year earlier when the *Regents' Prayer* decision was handed down. There was some of the damning language which followed the earlier decision. Congressman O'Konski (R. Wis.), for example, suggested mental tests for the Justices, and Senator Ellender (D. La.), continuing a long standing quarrel with the Court, referred to the "eight silly old men." [20] Senator Thurmond (D. S.C.) called it "another major triumph of secularism and atheism which are bent on throwing God completely out of our national life," while his colleague Senator Robertson (D. Va.) insisted that "we will become as Godless a nation as is the Soviet Union." [21] Striking a more positive note, Senator Johnston (D. S.C.) urged teachers to defy the decisions, and Congressman Ashmore (D. S.C.) moved that "In God We Trust" be placed in the Supreme Court building in much the same spirit that had led the House to place that motto behind the Speaker's desk a year earlier.[22] By and large, however, the violent outburst which had followed *Engel* was missing.

But whatever personal views members of Congress may have held, those of their constituents were made increasingly clear by a barrage of letters and petitions heavily weighted against the prayer and Bible reading decisions. And this unusually heavy flood of mail was soon followed by Congressional action in the form of numerous bills proposing amendments to the Constitution intended to reverse the *Schempp* decision. A comparison of Tables 1 and 2 indicates that almost twice as many members of Congress felt impelled to introduce such amendments as had been the case after *Engel*. In all, 146 amendments were introduced as of March 24, 1964. We are thus

20. Arnold Forster (Director of civil liberties division, ADL), *Memorandum to All ADL Regional Offices,* July 11, 1963, p. 6.
21. *Ibid.*
22. *Ibid.*

Table 2 [23]

PARTY AFFILIATION OF AUTHORS OF CONSTITUTIONAL AMENDMENTS TO
REVERSE *Schempp*. 88TH CONGRESS, 2D SESSION.

Party Affiliation	House	Senate
Republicans	64	15
Southern Democrats	30	8
Non-Southern Democrats	19	4
Total	113	27

faced with an interesting paradox: popular reaction to *Engel* was much greater than the outcry after *Schempp;* yet at the same time positive political action was much more significant after *Schempp* than it had been a year earlier. Several factors may help us to understand this situation. First, as indicated above, the 1963 decisions directly affected a much wider segment of the American public than had the *Regents' Prayer* case. Thus while the immediate outcry from public figures may have been greater after *Engel,* the *Schempp* decision was much more likely to stir up a widespread wave of opposition. Second, while it was not likely that Congressional action in response to *Engel* could have been taken in time to affect the 1962 Congressional elections, the elections of 1964 were constantly in the minds of Congressmen as Congress convened after the summer 1963 recess. And finally, we must interject into the 1963/64 situation the effects of the untiring efforts of Congressman Frank Becker (R. N.Y.).

Although the Senate had chosen to act following *Engel,* through its Judiciary Committee, the House was to be the center of the fight between supporters and opponents of amendments following *Schempp.* And the battle focused increasingly on the efforts of Representative Becker to push through such an amendment, and those

23. "Southern Democrats" represent the 11 states of the former Confederacy. The table is based on the *Congressional Record,* 88th Congress, both sessions. One might have expected many Southerners would have introduced such resolutions. It is important to realize that the pattern of behavior among Southern Congressmen was far from uniform. As indicated below, there were Southern states in which resentment against the Court would be expected to be high, in which the Congressmen did not feel called upon to introduce such amendments.

of Representative Emmanuel Celler (D. N.Y.), powerful chairman
of the House Judiciary Committee, to forestall any attack on the
Court's ruling. Becker had proposed an amendment after *Engel,* and
on the day after the 1963 decision was handed down, he introduced
another. Firmly convinced that the Court had struck a serious blow
against the religious training of the nation's youth, Becker devoted
all his personal efforts to a crusade to convince the public and his
colleagues that the great majority of Americans favored and were
entitled to the continuation of religious ceremonies in the public
schools. A devout Catholic, Congressman Becker had been educated

Table 3

NUMBER OF CONGRESSMEN INTRODUCING AMENDMENTS TO REVERSE
Schempp. 88TH CONGRESS, 1ST & 2D SESSIONS.

State	Democrats	Republicans
Alabama	3 out of 8	—
Arkansas	0 out of 4	—
Florida	5 out of 10	1 out of 2
Georgia	3 out of 10	—
Louisiana	1 out of 8	—
Mississippi	5 out of 5	—
North Carolina	7 out of 7	2 out of 2
South Carolina	4 out of 6	—
Tennessee	0 out of 3	3 out of 3
Texas	2 out of 19	0 out of 2
Virginia	0 out of 6	2 out of 2
Total	30 out of 86	8 out of 11

Note that almost all Southern Republicans introduced "anti-Court" amendments. But compare the behavior of Congressmen from Mississippi and North
Carolina with that of Democrats from Virginia and Arkansas. The authors
attempted to correlate the above indicated pattern with such factors as V. O.
Key's "Black Belt" thesis; income distribution; presence of an opposition party;
and religious affiliation of both Congressmen and population, without success.
Whatever caused this interesting pattern, it warns us to avoid the danger of
viewing the South monolithically in this matter.

in public schools, as had his children, and he regarded as wholly
salutary the modest practices by which the public schools recognized
the roles of God and of religion. Becker's zeal was reinforced by his
conception of the opponents he was combatting: "I certainly believe

that the atheists intend to bury religion. . . ." [24] Since he did not intend to seek re-election in 1964, Becker was prepared to devote virtually his entire energies to the task at hand. He made numerous public addresses, carried on a heavy correspondence, and made himself available as a leader in the fight to get an amendment through both Houses of Congress. Recognizing that the Chairman of the Judiciary Committee was unalterably opposed to any such amendment and would not let such a bill out of his committee unless compelled to do so, Becker sought to unite those who agreed with him on one form of amendment, and, by introducing a discharge petition either to force the holding of hearings, or to get his amendment out of Celler's committee and to the floor, where he anticipated favorable action by the required two-thirds of the House. With the unprecedented number of almost 115 fellow amendment seekers, he thought his chances of success were high, since only 218 signatures were necessary to discharge the bill from the committee. Becker faced two major difficulties from the start: one was the ingrained reluctance of many members to sign a discharge petition on any subject, particularly where the powerful Judiciary Committee was involved, the other was the coincidence of this issue and the Civil Rights Bill, eventually enacted in 1964, which tended to divide supporters of a prayer amendment.[25]

The bill which was to become identified in the public's mind as the "Becker Amendment" was not the bill introduced originally by the Representative, but was the product of a drafting effort by six members of Congress designated to perform this task following a meeting of amendment supporters in late August, 1963.[26] The amendment proposed in House Joint Resolution 693, introduced on September 10, 1963, provided that:

---

24. *Hearings on School Prayers Before the House Committee on the Judiciary*, 88th Cong., 2d Sess. 2008 (1964) [hereinafter cited as *1964 House Hearings*].
25. Note that the battle over Becker's discharge petition probably hurt the attempt to discharge the Civil Rights Bill from the House Rules Committee at about the same time. Many Congressmen who were afraid to "fight God" but who opposed Becker refused to sign his petition on the grounds that as a matter of principle they never signed discharge petitions. This prevented some from signing the civil rights discharge petition.
26. RNS, Aug. 26, 1963. The six were Becker, W. Baring (D. Nev.), W. Cramer (R. Fla.), D. Fuqua (D. Fla.), H. R. Kornegay (D. N.C.), and D. Latta (R. Ohio).

Sec. 1. Nothing in this Constitution shall be deemed to prohibit the offering, reading from, or listening to prayers or Biblical scriptures, if participation therein is on a voluntary basis, in any governmental or public school, institution or place.

Sec. 2. Nothing in this Constitution shall be deemed to prohibit making reference to, belief in, reliance upon, or invoking the aid of God or a Supreme Being in any governmental or public document, proceeding, activity, ceremony, school, institution, or place, or upon any coinage, currency, or obligation of the United States.

Sec. 3. Nothing in this article shall constitute an establishment of religion.

Ratification by three-fourths of the state legislatures within seven years was required by the last section of the proposed amendment.

During this period petitions and letters continued to pile up in congressional offices, and especially in those of members of the House Judiciary Committee. The campaign on behalf of an amendment to overcome the Court's decisions now had a clearer focus. From now on the battle was to be waged exclusively in terms of the Becker Amendment.

Although the volume of mail favoring the Becker Amendment continued to mount and members of the House continued to sign Becker's discharge petition, supporters of the decision did not view the matter seriously. The natural congressional opposition to discharge petitions under any circumstances and the feeling that the Judiciary Committee and especially its chairman could not be stampeded, along with the relative mildness of the initial reactions to the 1963 decision, led usually well-informed observers to believe that the Becker Amendment would peacefully die in committee. But support for the amendment from constituents of all types continued to mount, largely as a result of the activities of Congressman Becker and of organizations supporting his position. The *New York Times* reported that "largely through his efforts, it is conceded widely in Congress that Congressional mail on this issue has grown to flood proportions, exceeding the mail of the civil rights controversy." [27] Congressman Lionel Van Deerlin (D. Cal.) wrote that his colleagues "are being inundated with constituent mail, the great bulk of which favors such an amendment." [28] A form letter used by Congressman R. G. Ste-

27. N. Y. Times, April 23, 1964, p. 14, col. 5.
28. Personal letter to Mr. Dore Schary, in the ADL files.

phens (D. Ga.) to reply to constituents apologized for the fact that a printed reply was being used, but said that it was necessitated by the fact that he had had over one thousand letters on the subject. On February 18, the House Republican Policy Committee voted to support the Becker Amendment.[29] Congressman Alec G. Olson (D. Minn.) informed a constituent that he believed "this is a result of the large volume of mail running in favor of this amendment. In my case, I have received correspondence which is at least 200 to 1 in favor of such an amendment. . . ."[30] Gradually the number of signatures on the discharge petition rose so that eventually it contained almost 170 names.[31] And, the *Wall Street Journal* reported, "it is no secret that many more members including some hostile to the proposal and others adverse to the irregular procedure, have warned Mr. Celler that pressure from home would force them to sign unless he made some move."[32]

How is it that the members of Congress—who were surely well aware that much of the mail they were receiving was "inspired" —were sensitive to public sentiment to the extent that the *Wall Street Journal* pointed out that "for the most part, even lawmakers adamant in their opposition have kept silent in public"?[33] The answer is probably to be found in the way the issue was phrased by Becker and his supporters. In an election year, no Congressman wanted to be placed in a position of appearing to vote against God, which was exactly the role into which supporters of the Court were being forced. . . .

Early in 1964 it became apparent that Congressman Celler would have to schedule hearings, in order to avoid having the bill taken out of his committee. And indeed, by the middle of February he reacted to the Republican Policy Committee's demand for hearings by dryly

29. N. Y. Times, Feb. 19, 1964, p. 21, col. 3.

30. Letter to Mr. Merrill Keller, St. Paul, Minn., March 13, 1964, in ADL files.

31. It is impossible to know exactly how many signatures appear on a discharge petition at a given moment, as this figure is never officially released, and members can withdraw their names at any time. The *Wall Street Journal* reported that 166 signatures were said to have been obtained. This appears to square with other published reports, and with Becker's claims. Wall Street Journal, April 22, 1964, p. 1, col. 4.

32. *Id.* at 1.

33. *Ibid.*

remarking that a staff study was in progress, and that hearings would be scheduled when it was completed.[34] Opponents of the Becker Amendment who had previously been relatively inactive suddenly realized that if they did not stop Becker's juggernaut at the Committee hearings, their worst fears would be fulfilled. Meeting in New York on St. Patrick's Day, 1964, an *ad hoc* committee consisting of representatives of numerous Protestant, Jewish, and civil liberties groups opposed to the amendment decided that at that time the Becker Amendment had an excellent chance of receiving the approval of a majority of the Judiciary Committee, that if reported out favorably it was likely to pass easily in the House, and that while the Senate might delay passage of the bill, it would eventually pass there as well, an estimate concurred in by close students of the situation not present at the meeting.

Faced with this prospect, the members of the *ad hoc* group decided to coordinate their organizational efforts. It was agreed that probably the most important function the group could play would be to mobilize leaders of the religious community to oppose the Becker Amendment, in order to make it "respectable" and "safe" for Congressmen to oppose the Becker proposal. . . .

*   *   *

Although any effort to summarize briefly or evaluate the testimony of the contending forces is inevitably highly subjective, a few observations reflecting the authors' impressions may be of some value. The arguments of the Becker supporters followed the pattern previously established: the people favor such practices; the Court's decisions are an attack on God and on religion; this country was founded on a belief in God, and cannot exist without it; majorities have rights, and they need not always bow to the will of an "atheistic" minority.

*   *   *

Equally impressive, and perhaps almost as significant, was the testimony of legal scholars who attacked the amendment. . . .

34. N. Y. Times, Feb. 19, 1964, p. 21, col. 5.

The testimony of the opponents of the amendment was intended to sway the opinion of wavering congressmen. Which version of the *Bible* would be used? Would the *Koran* qualify under the amendment? Who would decide which prayers to say? Could the "Ave Maria" be employed? And again and again they returned to the basic theme: "thou shalt not touch the Bill of Rights."

The Becker Amendment movement, while endorsed widely, was essentially a one-man crusade. Although various organizations lent their support, and vigorous statements were made by several witnesses, the strategy used and the calibre of the witnesses did not match the efforts of the anti-amendment forces. To one who tries to read the pro-Becker testimony objectively, it seems that in the minds of many witnesses popular support for continuance of school prayers and Bible reading was regarded as the decisive factor. With notable exceptions, such as Charles Wesley Lowry,[35] many pro-Becker witnesses seemed to have adopted the simple equation—The people want prayers in schools; the Court took them away; we, on behalf of the people, must restore them. When the Chairman or other Committee members attempted to draw them out as to the effects of the various provisions of the amendment, they were often unable to follow the subtleties of the questioner. They frequently seemed annoyed by the complexities of issues framed by opponents.

Press coverage of the hearings was relatively full, and though the public was unable to gain a very coherent notion of the trend of the debates, it appears that the testimony of the anti-Becker church leaders and that of the legal authorities opposing the measure dominated the reports, especially in the later sessions. This may help to explain the increase in the anti-Becker mail, and a number of editorials throughout the nation urging that the amendment not pass.[36]

The real test of the effectiveness of the opposition lay in the impact on members of the Judiciary Committee. Although any judgment must be made with considerable reservation, it would seem that the direction of change of views of committee members was almost exclusively in one direction—against the amendment. At the beginning of the hearings, as noted above, the *ad hoc* committee had

35. *1964 House Hearings*, 1125.
36. See, *e.g.*, N. Y. Herald Tribune, May 10, 1964, p. 22, col. 1, editorial entitled "It's not a vote against God."

estimated that the Becker Amendment would easily win a majority in the committee; by the end of May, they expected that the Becker Amendment would probably be opposed by as many as 20 of the 35 members. By that time it was doubtful that any amendment then in prospect could attract a majority of the committee. It was apparent that the drive for a discharge petition had passed its crest; not only could it not gain the necessary 218 signatures, but members who had signed the petition were prepared to remove their names should the total approach 210. And even if a bill were discharged, it was doubtful that it could obtain a majority in the House, much less the required two-thirds majority. The *Wall Street Journal* doubted that as many as 8 members of the committee still supported an amendment.[37]

The use of public hearings as a means of shaping the thinking of committee members has been increasingly discounted by political analysts in recent years. They have tended to view them as a show with little relevance to the actual struggle over important public issues. The Becker Amendment hearings would appear to cast serious doubt as to the validity of these conclusions, for, as we have seen, the hearings had a significant impact *both* on Congressional opinion and on public opinion. The Becker hearings point to many aspects of the legislative process which students of future contests would do well to keep in mind. A combination of factors: expert, if belated, planning by opponents; their ability to gain the support of heavier "guns" at the hearings; and the natural advantage that our political system provides those opposing legislative action, was all too much for the Becker cause, regardless of its popular support. Also, the skillful operation of an experienced committee chairman and ally was of inestimable value to the anti-amendment forces.

* * *

37. Wall Street Journal, June 16, 1964, p. 3, col. 2.

STUART S. NAGEL

Court-Curbing Periods in American History

Due to its unavoidable involvement in the political process, the Supreme Court has often been an object of congressional attack. Excellent descriptive studies have been made of certain periods of conflict between Congress and the Court,[1] but there is a lack of writing which systematically analyzes relations between Congress and the Court throughout American history. It is the purpose of this paper to analyze in a partially quantitative manner some of the factors which seem to account for the occurrence or nonoccurrence and for the success or failure of congressional attempts to curb the Court.

I. RESEARCH DESIGN

One hundred and sixty-five instances of bills designed to curb the Supreme Court were compiled along with information concerning their content, sponsor, and fate from a perusal of *The Congressional Record* and its forerunners and also from the previous literature in the field.[2] In order to keep the data within manageable limits, reso-

1. Walter F. Murphy concentrates on the problems of the Warren Court in his book, CONGRESS AND THE COURT (1962) as does PRITCHETT, CONGRESS VERSUS THE COURT (1960). Robert Jackson concentrates on the 1937 Court-packing plan in THE STRUGGLE FOR JUDICIAL SUPREMACY: A STUDY OF A CRISIS IN AMERICAN POWER POLITICS (1941). . . .

2. *Ibid.* See also Culp, *A Survey of Proposals to Limit or Destroy the Power of Judicial Review by the Supreme Court of the United States*, 4 IND. L.J. 386,

From the *Vanderbilt Law Review*, 18: 3 (June 1965), pp. 925–44. Reprinted by permission of the publisher and the author.

Stuart S. Nagel is an Associate Professor of Political Science at the University of Illinois (Urbana).

lutions and constitutional amendments were not included although they are introduced frequently and often contain proposals which would substantially reduce the powers of the Court.[3] Relatively narrow bills designed to reverse a single decision were also excluded. Relying on the distribution of bills as well as the consensus of historians, seven time periods as shown in Table 1 were labeled high-frequency Court-curbing periods. This identification is both quantitative and qualitative. For example, the first period covering the years from 1802 to 1804, had only two instances of overt congressional attempts to curb the Court, one of which was the unsuccessful impeachment of Justice Chase. While it may well be a quantitatively marginal period, most writers agree that this was a time of high friction between the Federalists on the bench and the Jeffersonians in Congress and the Administration.

Table 1

HIGH AND LOW FREQUENCY PERIODS OF COURT-CURBING IN AMERICAN HISTORY

High-Frequency				Low-Frequency		
Years	# of Bills	% of 165		Years	# of Bills	% of 165
1. 1802–1804	2	1%	1.	1789–1801	0	0%
2. 1823–1831	12	7	2.	1805–1822	0	0
3. 1858–1869	22	13	3.	1832–1857	1	1
4. 1893–1897	9	5	4.	1870–1892	8	5
5. 1922–1924	11	7	5.	1898–1921	6	4
6. 1935–1937	37	22	6.	1925–1934	2	1
7. 1955–1957	53	32	7.	1939–1954	2	1
Total:	146	87%			19	12%

474 (1929); Warren, *The Early History of the Supreme Court of the United States in Connection with Modern Attacks on the Judiciary*, 8 MASS. L.Q. 1 (1922).

3. Twenty-five joint resolutions were proposed in 1937 while thirty-three constitutional amendments were introduced during the two year period from 1935 to 1937. Several attempts have been made, for example in 1867 and 1871, to establish via Constitutional amendment a new court representing all the states which would have jurisdiction over constitutional questions. A joint resolution in 1861 demanded the abolition of the federal judicial system.

A criterion by which to judge the relative success or failure of any one Court-curbing period is more difficult to establish. A total of only nine out of the 165 bills regulating the Court have passed Congress. This group of "absolutely successful" bills, representing approximately five per cent of the total instances, is too small to work with for the purposes of this study. Three criteria of "relative success" will therefore be used. First, *how many* anti-Court bills during each period were reported from committee, the lowest stage of the legislative process aside from introduction? Second, *what per cent* of the bills introduced were reported out of committee? The third criterion of success, as shown in Table 2, is that of determining whether a congressional attack has had the effect of changing within the immediate future the pattern of voting behavior of the Court on the issues which originally provoked the attack. In four of the seven attacks, the Court did retreat from its previous controversial policy by executing a tactical abstention from further similar provocation (as was the case in the years following the 1804 conflict) or by effecting a reversal of policy (as was the case in 1937). At the climax of the seventh period, the Court drew back from its stand on one of the issues which antagonized Congress—namely a broad interpretation of free speech —but remained firm on its policies toward segregation and criminal procedure which were also under congressional fire.

Table 2

RELATIVE SUCCESS OF SEVEN HIGH-FREQUENCY COURT-CURBING PERIODS

Years	Number of Bills Out of Committee	Per cent of Bills Out of Committee	Judicial Retreat	Composite Success	Rank Order of Composite Success
1. 1802–04	1	50%	Yes	Yes	3
2. 1823–31	3	25	Yes	Yes	4
3. 1858–69	11	50	Yes	Yes	1
4. 1893–97	1	11	No	No	7
5. 1922–24	2	18	No	No	6
6. 1935–37	6	16	Yes	Yes	2
7. 1955–59	2	4	Partial	No	5
	Avg. = 3.7 (N = 26)	Avg. 25% per period	Usually Yes	Usually Yes	

The fourth column in Table 2 provides a composite index of over-all success. Thus, a high-frequency period can be considered success-ful if it is above average on the number of bills that were reported out of committee (*i.e.,* four or more); if it is above average on the per cent of successful bills (*i.e.,* 25% or above); and if it was cli-maxed by retreat of the Court on the majority of the issues involved. A period will be termed relatively successful if it is above average on at least two of these three criteria. Using this composite standard, four of the seven high-frequency periods have been classified as rela-tive overall successes, and each period has been given a rough success ranking as shown in the last column of Table 2.

The variables influencing the occurrence and success of the seven Court-curbing periods seem to fit into a model like the psychological model of stimulus-organism-response. In the political phenomenon of Court-curbing, the stimulus is represented by judicial provocation. The organism is represented by the political system which may con-tain certain catalytic or conditioning factors which shape the percep-tion of the provocation and the response. The response manifests itself in certain types of Court-curbing bills and Presidential action. This response may feed back on the judiciary and thereby stimulate judicial counter-action. Having this overall model in mind helps one to see better the interrelations between the more specific variables discussed in this paper.

II. JUDICIAL PROVOCATION

A. *Quantity of Judicial Review*

To what extent does a high quantity of judicial review of legislative acts provoke Court-curbing regardless of the type of interests in-volved? Table 3 shows that almost 50 of the total 86 instances of judicial nullification of federal statutes in American history have occurred during or within three years prior to the seven Court-curbing periods. Thus, over half of the instances of judicial nulli-fication have occurred during a time span equaling less than one-third of the history of the Supreme Court. The use of judicial review for the first time in *Marbury v. Madison*,[4] was certainly an irritant in the Federalist-Jeffersonian dispute over relative amounts of judicial and executive power in the early 1800's. The nullification of state bankruptcy and debtor laws as well as the invalidation of a Maryland act taxing the Bank of the United States provoked the wrath of congressmen in the 1820's.[5] The 1858 Dred Scott case [6] nullified a federal statute, and congressional anticipation of judicial review of Reconstruction legislation led to the court-packing and restrictions on habeas corpus in the 1860's. The 1890's attack was precipitated in part by the invalidation of a federal income tax law, and nullification of federal and state economic legislation led to another Progressive attack on the Court in the 1920's. The judicial review of fifteen New Deal statutes was a prime causative factor in the 1930's conflict. In the 1950's, portions of federal and state laws were held unconstitutional, and proposed legislation such as the Jenner bill was clearly aimed at several decisions. In short, all the periods of intense Court-curbing have been provoked to some degree by the judicial review of legislative acts. Nullification of federal statutes, however, seems to provide a greater provocation than nullification of state statutes since judicial review of state statutes seemed to be a prime factor only in

Table 3

OCCURRENCE OF JUDICIAL REVIEW DURING AND 3 YEARS PRIOR TO THE
HIGH-FREQUENCY COURT-CURBING PERIODS

Years	Instances of judicial review of federal acts during or 3 years prior
1802–04	1
1823–31	0 *
1858–69	5
1893–97	3
1922–24	13
1935–37	15
1955–59	5
Total:	42

* Judicial review of state acts present
4. 5 U.S. (1 Cranch) 137 (1803).
5. 17 U.S. (4 Wheat.) 316 (1819).
6. 60 U.S. (19 How.) 393 (1857).

the 1820's Court-curbing period and partially in the 1950's. Congress is apparently more protective of its own lawmaking than it is of the various state legislative bodies.

If the seven periods are divided into the periods of relatively high judicial review of federal legislation and relatively low . . . a slightly greater proportion of the relatively high review periods involved relatively successful Court-curbing bills than did the relatively low review periods. Thus, the intensity of judicial review may be a partial determinant of the success of controversial Court-curbing bills as well as a determinant of the introduction of Court-curbing bills. There are, however, more important determinants of Court-curbing success as will be shown later.

B. *Subject of the Provoking Cases*

The specific issues over which conflict has occurred whether from judicial review cases or other cases can be divided into four categories —economic regulation, civil liberties, federal-state relations, and general separation of powers. Table 4 indicates that first, economic regulation has been involved to some extent in four of the seven high-frequency periods. Civil liberties and federal-state relations have each been at issue in two periods, while general separation of powers at the national level has been the main controversy in only the earliest period.

Trends in the frequency or occurrence of certain issues are apparent. For example, the attacks during the first half of the nineteenth century were largely concerned with federal-state relations and separation of powers, a fact which can be explained in part by the youth of the country. At this time, the power distribution between the parts of the newly established federal system was not at all clear, this question being a dividing point between the two political parties as well as a major public issue. From the latter half of the nineteenth century through 1937, the basic issue in Congress-court relations was that of economic regulation. Conflict over civil liberties has occurred intermittently but particularly in recent years.

From the data in Table 4 one might also be able to say that Court-curbing bills are more likely to succeed where federal-state relations

Table 4
INTERESTS INVOLVED IN COURT-CURBING DURING AMERICAN HISTORY

Issues	Period	Overall Success
1. Economic Interests		
a. Business Regulation	1930's	Yes
	1890's	No
	1820's	Yes
b. Labor Relations	1890's	No
	1920's	No
c. Taxes	1890's	No
2. Civil Liberties		
a. Segregation	1950's	No
b. First Amendment	1950's	Partial
	1860's	Yes
c. Criminal Procedure	1950's	No
	1860's	Yes
3. Federal-State Relations		
	1800's	Yes
	1820's	Yes
4. Separation of Powers in the National Government	1800's	Yes

or separation of powers represent the prime subject matters involved. On the other hand, where intensely held economic interests or civil libertarian interests are involved, the likelihood of Court-curbing success is decreased.

C. *Unanimity of Provoking Cases*

Does the degree of conflict within the Supreme Court influence the occurrence of congressional Court-curbing? The degree of conflict within the Court can be measured by the degree of unanimity in key decisions at a given time. Using the statements of various writers and congressmen as to what cases provoked the anti-Court bills, the voting split on these controversial decisions was determined. The average degree of unanimity for all the periods was 76% which means that there was an average of two to three dissents in the cases provoking the attacks. This number contrasts with the higher degree of unanimity normally found in the totality of Supreme Court cases. The results of Table 5 support the hypothesis that during periods in which there is a relatively high (*i.e.*, above average) degree of disagreement between members of the Court (and thus high controversy), congressional attack is more likely to occur.

Table 5

DEGREE OF UNANIMITY IN THE SUPREME COURT AND THE EFFECT ON
OCCURRENCE AND SUCCESS OF COURT-CURBING

Periods	Degree of Unanimity		Relative Success
1800's	100%	relatively high	Yes
1820's	89	rel. high	Yes
1860's	59	rel. low	Yes
1890's	72	rel. low	No
1920's	69	rel. low	No
1930's	69	rel. low	Yes
1950's	76	rel. high	No
	Avg. = 76%		

Contrary to what one might expect Table 5 shows that a slightly greater proportion of the high unanimity (rather than the low unanimity) periods involved relatively successful Court-curbing bills. However, the high unanimity in the 1800's and the 1820's does not necessarily indicate complete unity on the part of the Court. It may merely indicate that dissenting had not yet become an established practice.

*   *   *

III. CONGRESSIONAL AND PRESIDENTIAL RESPONSE

A. *Congressional Response*

Several courses of action are available to the congressmen seeking to attack the policies of the Supreme Court. At the local level, he can participate in nullification movements to register disapproval of a particular decision. In Congress, he can attempt retaliation via the fiscal powers, introduce restrictive constitutional amendments, sponsor legislation to overturn a statutory interpretation, initiate joint resolutions or investigations, or, if a Senator, he can attempt to block a Presidential nominee for the bench. Although these methods account for a good share of the activity during congressional attacks on the Court, this paper and the following table is concerned only with specific bills designed directly or indirectly to change some general policy of the Court.

Table 6

TYPES OF BILLS PROPOSED TO CURB THE SUPREME COURT

	Frequency		Relative Success	
	Number	% of 165	Number	% of Type
1. Judicial Review				
a. Special concurrence needed	41	25%	5	12%
b. Miscellaneous regulate	5	3	0	0
c. Abolish	3	2	0	0
Total:	49	30%	5	10% Avg.
2. Personnel				
a. Qualifications	24	15	0	0
b. Size of Court	13	8	5	38
c. Retirement	7	4	3	43
d. Appointing	4	2	1	25
e. Give states equal representation	1	½	0	0
Total:	49	29½%	9	18% Avg.
3. Jurisdiction				
a. Regulate and define general appellate jurisdiction	23	14	3	13
b. Repeal Supreme Court jurisdiction over state	3	2	1	33
c. Limit jurisdiction in special cases:				
1) Habeas corpus appeals	3	2	2	67
2) Reconstruction	1	½	0	0
3) Public schools	7	4	0	0
4) Other specific areas	8	5	1	12
Total:	45	27½%	7	16% Avg.

Table 6 (*continued*)

TYPES OF BILLS PROPOSED TO CURB THE SUPREME COURT

	Frequency		Relative Success	
	Number	% of 165	Number	% of Type
4. Procedure				
a. General reorganization	6	4	3	50
b. Amend judicial code	4	2	2	50
c. Amend rules of practice and procedure	1	½	0	0
d. Facilitate decisions on constitutional questions	1	½	0	0
Total:	12	7%	5	42% Avg.
5. Curtail Contempt or Injunction Powers	4	2	3	75
6. Miscellaneous				
a. Let lower court ignore non-legalistic Sup. Ct. decisions	2	1	0	0
b. Change doctrine of pre-emptive federalism	1	½	1	100
c. Postpone meeting of Court	1	½	1	100
d. Impeachment	1	½	1	100
e. Give some body direct review over Sup. Ct. decisions	1	½	0	0
Overall Total:	165	100%	32	19% Avg.

After the congressman has decided to attack the power of the judges and to do it through legislative means, he still has a range of alternatives from which to choose. Table 6 indicates that about 30% of the Court-curbing bills dealt with regulating or abolishing judicial review which particularly includes bills requiring special concurrences to declare statutes unconstitutional. Another 29% dealt with matters of Court personnel, particularly qualifications (like lengthy prior judicial experience) for holding a Supreme Court judgeship. Within this 29% are also included thirteen bills designed to increase or decrease the size of the Court so as to allow a new President to make new appointments or to keep him from making new appointments. About 28% of the bills attempted to restrict the court's appellate jurisdiction, and the relatively few remaining bills dealt with various procedural and miscellaneous matters.

Some measures have been peculiar to one time period. Bills curtailing the contempt and injunction powers were predominant, for example, during the period of the Progressives' attack on the Court, particularly before the enactment of the Clayton Act.[7] Bills pertaining to the appellate jurisdiction of the Court in respect to public schools, and bills abolishing the doctrine of pre-emptive federalism were characteristic of the 1955–1959 conflict. The broad historic trend has been away from bills which would remove or circumscribe a broad area of the Court's power and toward those bills which would limit a small, more specific part of the Court's functions. For example, the only serious attempt at impeachment occurred in 1804. Bills advocating the repeal of the 25th section of the Judiciary Act of 1789 which would be tantamount to removing the Court's appellate jurisdiction over state courts were concentrated in the first half of the nineteenth century. Unsuccessful bills providing for equal representation of the states on the Court were proposed prior to 1870, and thus those groups favoring such a change have recently resorted to a constitutional amendment via a constitutional convention. In contrast, many bills proposed during the intense conflict in 1937 were designed to effect changes in the quorum, retirement of Justices, and size of the Court. In the attack on the Warren Court, many bills prescribed limitation of jurisdiction in special cases dealing with subversion, public schools, and (after 1961) reapportionment. More extreme bills in the earlier years may be attributable to the fact that in the early nineteenth century, the rule of the judicial branch of the government was not yet established, and the obvious partisanship of some justices during the very early years was a hindrance to the growth of the judicial myth. In addition, history has shown that bills removing comparatively smaller amounts of the Court's power have the greatest prospect of success. Astute congressmen may well have taken note of this fact. One, however, should note that although the severity of bills during the Warren and Roosevelt courts was lower than in prior periods, the quantity of bills was higher. This possibly indicated a more widespread discontent toward specific decisions and a lack of cohesive leadership by the anti-Court forces which kept these forces from centering on one or a few bills.

7. 64 Stat. 1125 (1950), 15 U.S.C. § 12 (1958).

With regard to the matter of success, ten of the twenty-three categories of bills had a higher percentage of relative success (*i.e.,* got out of committee) than the average of 19%. These ten types of bills included repealing jurisdiction over state supreme courts, limiting jurisdiction in regard to habeas corpus appeals, changing the rules concerning retirement and the size of the Court, restricting the Court's procedure, and limiting the Court's contempt and injunction powers. Most of the ten types could be considered as limited means of curbing the Court. The substantially higher rate of success for the relatively milder bills can be explained by the fact that during all the time periods, there has been a sizeable opposition in Congress to any attempts to curb the Supreme Court—a factor which necessitates compromise.

B. *Presidential Response*

To what extent have Presidents become involved in Court-curbing and what effect has their participation had on the outcome of congressional court conflicts? Four Presidents have been openly critical of the Court during the high-frequency periods, *i.e.,* Jefferson, Jackson, Lincoln, and Roosevelt, but not Eisenhower or the Presidents of the 1920's or 1890's. Presidents have been hesitant to openly initiate Court-curbing legislation. FDR's Court-packing plan of 1937 was an exception, but it was only one of numerous anti-Court bills introduced in the 1930's. This presidential reluctance is possibly due to a fear of alienating the Court's numerous defenders in Congress and the public (as well as a respect for the independence of the judiciary), and in some instances to a favorable presidential attitude toward the Court's policies.

With regard to the success of individual bills, Roosevelt's Court-packing bill was reported out of committee unfavorably. This is attributable to inadequate cultivation of support in Congress and among the public and to reversals by the Court itself. In view of the Court's retreat, however, the Roosevelt period can be considered a relative success. Presidents also have administrative weapons to either thwart or aid orders of the Supreme Court, and ultimately via his appointive power the President can change the Court's policies.

Nevertheless, with the astute use of his tools of leadership, the President can be a powerful figure both in the initiation and successful outcome of Court-curbing bills. With his active support Court-curbing legislation is probably more likely to pass, and without it, such legislation is more likely to fail.

*   *   *

HARRY P. STUMPF

The Political Efficacy of Judicial Symbolism

*   *   *

I

. . . [T]he Supreme Court in American society, which Arnold terms "our most important symbol of government," [1] continues to be regarded as the font of impartiality and legitimacy, of near-infallibility amidst the chaos of conflicting notions of legality. And even among those writers who are fond of emphasizing the policy-making or "political" role of the Court (often along with a description of its historical foibles) one is still likely to find references to the awe and reverence in which the Court is held—to the magic or sacrosanctity of the Court and its personnel. But the descriptive emphasis has now in large part shifted from the perpetuation of the myth that the judiciary *is* or should be infallible to the assertion that courts and judges are *regarded* as such by the body politic. This latter treatment of judicial mythology is often accompanied by attempts to assess its political significance. That is, the mystical quality of the judiciary is currently being treated as a political variable used in part to explain the political efficacy of courts, especially the United States Supreme Court. For example Murphy and Pritchett argue that the first reason

1. Thurman W. Arnold, *The Symbols of Government* (New Haven: Yale U. Press, 1935), p. 196.

From the *Western Political Quarterly*, 19: 2 (June 1966), pp. 293–303. Reprinted by permission of the University of Utah, copyright owners, and by permission of the author.

Harry P. Stumpf is Associate Professor of Political Science at the University of New Mexico.

judges are not ". . . throttled at the whim of other politicians" is that ". . . Courts are protected by their magic; only rarely can a hand be laid on a judge without a public outcry of sacrilege." [2] In addition, each of these scholars, in his effort to analyze the 1958 Court-Congress "crisis," suggests that the Court's prestige played a role in thwarting legislative threats to its powers. . . .

The difficulty with such familiar explanations is that their appealing plausibility has always seemed to preclude the necessity of empirical examination. Even in the absence of hard data, little if any disagreement is to be found with Max Lerner's observations that the Court "has a strong symbolic hold over the American mind," and that to the man in the street the Supreme Court is a symbol of "ancient sureness and a comforting stability." [3] Moreover, when this "sacrosanctity proposition" is more narrowly applied to explain specific judicial victories over congressional or presidential threats, there remains the propensity to accept such explanations as plain common sense. The argument here is not that courts have no symbolic appeal, nor that judicial magic cannot be employed to account for judicial power. Rather, assuming the "cult of the robe" to be a variable of some significance, the plea being made is to the need for more empirical data which could be marshaled to tell us something of the conditions under which this symbol is successfully invoked. To put the matter a little differently, if the empirical study of political symbolism represents a "highly promising" area for future research, as was recently claimed,[4] perhaps it is time to take a closer look at one of the most familiar of such symbols, that of the courts.

In terms of the degree of specificity, the assertion we have called the "sacrosanctity proposition" may be found on at least three levels. First, and at the highest level of generality, is the blanket declaration common to the Lerner article, simply that the Court is an important

2. Walter F. Murphy and C. Herman Pritchett, *Courts, Judges and Politics: An Introduction to the Judicial Process* (New York: Random House, 1961), pp. 554–55.
3. Max Lerner's "Constitution and Court as Symbols," though nearly thirty years old (46 *Yale L.J.* 1290–1319, June 1937), appears to be the most recent substantive research in judicial symbolism as a political variable.
4. Rollo Handy and Paul Kurtz, *A Current Appraisal of the Behavioral Sciences,* Section 4, *Political Science and Jurisprudence* (Great Barrington, Mass.: Behavioral Research Council, 1963), p. 67.

symbol of government. Included in the second level are statements of an explanatory nature exemplified by Pritchett's quotation above as well as by similar assertions in the Lerner essay. These seek to explain the outcome of broad-scale political activity or perhaps the perpetuation of long-standing doctrine or policy as a function of the symbolic influence enjoyed by the Supreme Court. Finally, at a more specific level of discourse, judicial symbolism has been employed to explain a slightly more narrow set of political relationships. . . . Schubert suggests . . . that one of the principal reasons that congressional reversal of statutory rulings is only infrequently successful is the invocation of the symbol of the prestige or sacrosanctity of the Court and/or its decisions. "Decisions . . . are themselves political data, and they provide strong ammunition for congressmen . . ."; and ". . . the argument that proponents of the amendatory bill are showing disrespect for the highest court in the land is an effective one." [5]

Using the Schubert statement as a point of departure—as a research datum—it appears that we are afforded a convenient, if limited, entry into the problem noted above. By testing the validity of this asserted relationship between the on-going process of the congressional reversal of the Court's statutory rulings [6] and the invocation of judicial prestige, it should be possible to shed some empirical light on the role of judicial symbolism, at least as concerns one facet of our national policy process.

II

If the proposition, even in this more narrow form, retains an acceptable degree of plausibility, the problem of testability still remains.

5. Glendon A. Schubert, *Constitutional Politics: The Political Behavior of Supreme Court Justices and the Constitutional Policies They Make* (New York: Holt, Rinehart & Winston, 1960), pp. 257–58.
6. The literature concerning this almost day-to-day legislative-judicial interaction process is scanty but growing. See especially "Congressional Reversal of Supreme Court Decisions, 1945–1957," 71 *Harvard L. Rev.* 1324–37 (May 1958) . . . and Harry P. Stumpf, "The Congressional Reversal of Supreme Court Decisions, 1957–1961" (Ph.D. dissertation, Northwestern University, 1964).

This writer is hardly the first to be troubled with vaguely worded statements of relationships. That such relationships in many cases, and certainly in this one, must be explicitly restated to permit empirical examination is clear. But the problem of an explication consistent with the original statement is ever present. Perhaps the best solution is to make perfectly clear one's step-by-step explication, then allow the reader to pass judgment on the fairness of the emerging hypothesis.

Schubert states, in effect, that congressional reversal of Supreme Court decisions is neither as easy nor as frequent as is popularly supposed due in part to the invocation of two symbols, the prestige or sacrosanctity of the Court itself and the integrity of the Court's decisions. Now if the use of such symbols is "effective" or "strong ammunition" which augurs against reversal, then it must produce results; and results here have meaning only in terms of the failure of proposed reversal legislation. In other words it would not do to say, on the one hand, that the use of these symbols is effective in defeating attempted reversals, but on the other hand there is no significant association between such use and the outcome of reversal bills. Hence, the proposition would seem to require a positive correlation between the independent variable, "use of stated symbol," and the dependent variable, "outcome of reversal bills." Assuming dichotomized data, the matrix might look like this:

	Symbol	
Bills	Absent	Present
Passed	XXXX	
Not Passed		XXXX

Matrix of Schubert Proposition, assuming dichotomized variables.

If one assumes "use of stated symbol" to mean use by congressmen, there is but one practical way to test the proposition, and that is by content analyzing House and Senate floor debate on those bills which would reverse Supreme Court decisions. Committee hearings might also be included except that testimony is largely by private or official spokesmen other than congressmen. A preliminary examination of such floor debate indicates that the independent variable "use of symbol" is not naturally dichotomous. That is to say, although use of such symbols is not present in all debate, there is present a certain level of use in numerous floor considerations which involve both passage and failure of subject bills. While it is clear that this fact immediately casts doubt on the validity of the proposition as stated, a fairer test might be drawn in terms of frequency of symbol usage. This can be justified by considering the implications of the original Schubert proposition. That is, can one say (1) use of the symbol is effective in stopping reversal bills, but (2) as use increases, results remain the same or become increasingly adverse? True, this may very well be the case, but the contrary is implied by the original proposition. Hence, after considering both the wording and the import of the Schubert statement as well as the nature of the data used in testing it, the original proposition may be formally restated in the following manner: *The higher the frequency of use of the sacrosanctity argument in Congress, the less likely is the reversal bill to pass.*

Reversal bill may be defined as proposed congressional legislation the intent or effect, or part of the intent or effect of which is to modify the legal result or impact, or perceived legal result or impact of a specific Supreme Court decision, or decisions.[7] But since for the above reasons the universe of data is to be limited to House and Senate floor debate on such proposals, a reversal bill must reach the stage of floor consideration to be included in the analysis. Given this, and using the five-year period of 1957 to 1961, Congress was found to have acted on forty-four reversal proposals relating to nineteen separate topics and directly involving some twenty-seven Supreme Court decisions. . . .[8]

"In Congress" refers to House and Senate floor debate on these reversal attempts as found in the *Congressional Record* for the five-

7. This definition is a slight modification of the one found in "Congressional Reversal of Supreme Court Decisions, 1945–1957," 73 *Harvard L. Rev.* 1324 (1958).

8. The reversal attempts during this five-year period were located by reference to a multitude of written sources as well as through consultation with several congressional committee staff members familiar with the process. Of the written

year period (Vols. 103–7). Using the Index of House Bills and Resolutions of each volume as an entry guide, the debate was content-analyzed in terms of the following categories:

Decision Themes—If Court decisions are "political data" and provide "strong ammunition for congressmen" and if this can be interpreted as referring to floor debate, then the pertinent decision(s) must be mentioned or referred to in such debate in a "favorable" vein. Examining the entirety of floor debate on these reversal bills, one finds that references to decisions of the Court almost always occur in complete sentences. For this reason the sentence was selected as the most suitable "context unit." [9] And if the aim of the research is to locate "favorable" references to subject decisions, the smallest body of debate content containing such references is the simple assertion, i.e., subject and predicate. The recording unit for the analysis thus becomes the assertion, or to use a more common term in content analysis, the theme. Such themes are included as indicators of the sacrosanctity argument if they refer to the decision(s) or companion decision(s) by identifying them with "good" words, ideas or symbols, or if they simply state agreement with the decisions. Typical examples of decision themes would be assertions that the decision is a sound statement of the law—a *great landmark*—it is a *fair, correct, realistic, effective* or an *American* decision, etc.

Court Themes—The sacrosanctity argument may also be found in court themes—generally, assertions by congressmen which are favorable or complimentary to the Court. Using the same context and recording units, court themes are found in the following categories: assertions expressing *trust, faith, confidence* in the judiciary, either past, present or future or assertions which assign *favorable ideas, terms* or *symbols* to the Court, its work or its personnel, i.e., the Court is the *irreplaceable guardian of our system of justice*, its members are *brilliant, distinguished*, etc. These indicators collectively define *court theme* and together with those of *decision theme* consti-

sources, the *Congressional Quarterly Almanac*, law review articles, both of a specialized nature as well as the annual survey articles, treatises in various fields of law, and the *Congressional Record* proved to be the most helpful. For a discussion of the substantive issues involved in these attempted reversals consult the author.

9. See Bernard Berelson, *Content Analysis in Communication Research* (Glencoe: Free Press, 1952), chap. V, wherein units of analysis are discussed.

tute a formal definition of "sacrosanctity argument," the key variable
of the hypothesis.[10]

III

*   *   *

Although it is apparent at a glance that the data tend toward a
disconfirmation of the hypothesis as tested, it might be well to
present this fact in matrix form. By dichotomizing the data of both
variables, the contingency table would be:

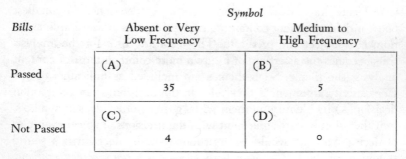

	Symbol	
Bills	Absent or Very Low Frequency	Medium to High Frequency
Passed	(A) 35	(B) 5
Not Passed	(C) 4	(D) 0

Matrix of Findings

Applying the Fisher Exact Probability Test, we have: [11]

$$p = \frac{(A+B)!\,(C+D)!\,(A+C)!\,(B+D)!}{N!\,A!\,B!\,C!\,D!} = 1.000000$$

10. For a more complete and detailed discussion of these indicators, consult
the author. In reply to the Berelson charge (p. 172) that reliability checks are
too infrequent in content analysis studies, a random sample of four debates was
used for a reliability check by a student who had at his disposal only the indicators listed herein. The results (tabulated below) indicate a very high level
of agreement, hence reliability.

	Original Findings (Themes)	Reliability Test Findings (Themes)
Interstate Taxation	2	2
Smith Act (Yates)	0	0
FBI Files (Jencks)	16	18
Sports	0	0

11. See Sidney Siegel, *Nonparametric Statistics for the Behavioral Sciences*
(New York: McGraw-Hill, 1956), pp. 96–104; and Helen M. Walker and

The probability, then, of observing this or a more extreme set of data in the direction of the hypothesis is 100 out of 100 times. That is, the data are purely chance and do not to any degree support the hypothesis; in fact, the weight of data could not be stronger to the contrary.

The findings raise the fundamental question of the relationship between the data and the original Schubert proposition. Even if the hypothesis is rejected, is it not still possible if not probable that the prestige or sacrosanctity of the Court and its decisions protect that body in some manner from the success of congressional reversal? Perhaps, but if the 1957–61 sample can be said to be at all representative, the data therefrom certainly suggest some revision of the Schubert language. We can no longer say that Court decisions provide "strong ammunition for congressmen" against proposed reversal bills, for in the overwhelming majority of debates on such bills (thirty-eight out of forty-four) not a voice was raised in this vein, and in the remaining six cases such arguments appeared to have had little or no effect in and of themselves in halting the passage of reversal legislation. Likewise, it is not quite accurate to term "effective" the argument that proponents of reversal legislation are showing disrespect for the Court when (1) very few such statements are ever made, at least on the floor of Congress (found in only seven of the forty-four reversal bill debates) and (2) even when these arguments were invoked, the bill was eventually passed. Such sacrosanctity arguments could be used in committee, in informal verbal interchange among congressmen or perhaps between congressmen and representatives of the various interest groups. But a close examination of committee hearings and reports on these bills reveals very few instances of such arguments. Moreover, it does not seem likely that congressmen who are proud of the Court and its decisions, interested in its welfare and anxious to defend it against reversal would invoke judicial symbolism in private but fail to do so in formal debate, especially if such arguments are effective in attaining their goals.

Perhaps a more plausible explanation or analysis of the findings herein would be that while the prestige or sacrosanctity of the Court and its decisions does indeed constitute an important barrier against

Joseph Lev, *Statistical Inference* (New York: Holt, 1953), pp. 103–6. The reasons for the selection of the Fisher Test rather than X^2 or a correlation formula are explained in these works.

legislative or even executive threats, one certainly cannot empirically demonstrate this fact by counting statements made or not made on the floor of Congress, or anywhere else for that matter. *Everybody knows*, continues the argument, that the Court's prestige is an important, if not *the* important ingredient of its power. After all, doesn't everyone remember how the FDR Court-packing (or unpacking) plan was defeated by a Congress which was "shocked" that anyone would lay hands upon an independent judiciary? The "everybody knows" explanation, then, suggests that while the sacrosanctity variable is an important one, it is seldom outwardly invoked; it is just there, like Rousseau's General Will, to watch over the Court and its decisions. Accordingly, Schubert did not mean to imply that the argument is literally used. Rather, he was referring to a subliminal condition. Hence, no one would expect the measuring device employed herein to reveal its presence. There are at least two difficulties with this explanation. First, it is not consistent with what Schubert said, and second, the number of decisions reversed by both houses of Congress (sixteen in all for the five-year period) indicates that the General Will was not operative on a good many occasions; otherwise, these bills would not have been passed.

Yet a third alternative explanation of (or around) the above findings would be that the reversal proposals considered herein were, in the main, innocuous ones which did not constitute serious threats to the Court or its prestige. More specifically, whereas "reversal bill" was here defined in terms of the decision only, Schubert may have been referring to legislation *anti-Court* in nature. Such legislation might fall into two broad categories: (1) anti-Court or Court-curbing bills having as their purpose, either expressed or implied, an alteration in the structure or functioning of the Supreme Court as an institution within the context of legislative-judicial conflict (i.e., H.R. 3 of 1956–61, the Jenner-Butler bill of 1957–58, legislation to alter the professional requirements for appointment to the Court, etc.) and (2) bills anti-Court in mood—legislation, that is, only anti-decision in wording but which occurs either within the context of or becomes symbolic of Court-Congress conflict.[12] Had this type of more threat-

---

12. See Walter F. Murphy, *Congress and the Court* (Chicago: U. of Chicago Press, 1962), p. 177, for a discussion of the 1958 habeas corpus legislation which is a typical example of a bill anti-Court in mood.

ening legislation been used for testing purposes, perhaps the study would have revealed a significant relationship between use of the sacrosanctity symbol and the outcome of these bills. Despite the fact that Schubert made no such distinction, it might be well to examine this possibility.

Since the instant research treats of decision reversal as opposed to Court-curb or anti-Court bills, no statement can be made with respect to (1) above. But the data do permit a check on the above explanation through the isolation of reversal bills in the anti-Court mood—bills which were in the mainstream of the 1957–59 Court-Congress "crisis." As explained in both the Murphy and Pritchett volumes as well as in several other items of the literature, this "crisis" related primarily to national security matters—questions of the proper role of the federal government in the area commonly known as subversive activities. This would clearly and directly include the decisions of *Jencks, Yates, Kent, Cole,* and *Greene,* and at least indirectly the *Mallory, Brown* (habeas corpus) and probably the deportation appeals cases. From the above interpretation of the Schubert statement one would expect that debate on bills to reverse these decisions would contain a higher number or rate of decision or Court themes than would debate on the remaining bills. But the data here are somewhat conflicting. Viewed from one angle, five of these eight reversal topics in the anti-Court mood category contain no such themes or symbols; hence, in this respect they differ not at all from the remaining topics. On the other hand (and this may prove to be significant) of 117 Court and decision themes recorded, 115 (98 per cent) were found in debate on bills in the anti-Court mood, especially the Jencks and Mallory bills.

Why, though, are the Jencks and Mallory reversals unique? After all, were not some of the other national security reversal bills equally in the anti-Court mood? From the verbatim debate on the Jencks and Mallory bills as well as from the discussions of these issues in the previously cited literature, it can be argued that the reversal proposals introduced in Congress on these two topics were perceived for varying reasons to be representative of the whole, or most, of the anti-Court sentiment of these years. Jencks came early in the struggle, and successful reversal here, congressional friends of the Court reasoned, would surely be followed by attempts to reverse other heavily

criticized Court decisions of the October 1956 term. Murphy tends
to support this analysis in his beginning discussion of the Jencks
bills. "While *Watkins, Yates, Sweezy, Service* and the bar admission
cases were all controversial as well as important decisions, newspaper,
congressional, and executive attention swiftly focused on *Jencks v.
United States* as the most dangerous precedent of the lot." [13] To an
even greater extent, the occasion of the floor consideration of the
Mallory bills, even though not strictly in the national security category, was seized upon by congressional "liberals" as a strategic point
from which to defend the Court. This is indicated by Pritchett in his
discussion of the Mallory issue, especially on pages 35–40, and in
his quotation of the comment of Senator Javits in the 1958 Mallory
debate. Javits remarked: "Were I not convinced . . . that this is but
the first bill dealing with dissatisfaction with decisions of the Supreme Court, and if I did not realize that the record made in connection with this measure will be a great indication to the country, as
well as to our colleagues, of how we think about the entire problem
raised by various decisions of the United States Supreme Court, I
would not make this presentation against the bill today." [14] By way
of contrast, the other bills in the anti-Court mood were either over-
shadowed in importance (not substantively, but strategically) by
Mallory and *Jencks* or came to the floor after the major battle was
over.

Returning to the original question of the relationship of the
Court's prestige to reversal of its decisions by Congress, it appears
that while the "ordinary" or "simple" reversal attempt—one, that is,
with no or little anti-Court overtone—is not related to the sacrosanctity symbol or even to the more general prestige of the Court, the
reversal proposal which either by general legislative context or possibly by actual content can be seen as anti-Court in character *is* so
related to the Court's prestige and its indicator, the sacrosanctity
argument. Certainly there is no evidence in the present data that use
of this symbol in debate on bills anti-Court in flavor or content in
and of itself inhibits their passage. Yet the fact that the anti-Court

13. *Ibid.*, p. 127.
14. C. Herman Pritchett, *Congress versus the Supreme Court* (Minneapolis:
U. of Minnesota Press, 1961), p. 36.

tone of a bill tends to provoke symbol usage does suggest that were the term "reversal bill" to be defined so as to include bills in the anti-Court and anti-Court mood categories, a significant relationship between symbol usage and success of such bills might very well emerge. At any rate future research on judicial symbolism should certainly investigate this possibility.

2 Impact on the Lower Courts

According to traditional theories of formal organizational structure, when a superior issues a command it is expected that the order will be carried out by those below speedily and faithfully. Present-day experience, however, seems to indicate that this theory does not hold much water. Even the tightest organization, wherein ultimate authority formally resides in a single person (e.g., the President), there are great discrepancies between what the superior says he wants done and what even his most loyal subordinates actually do. This is essentially what Richard Neustadt means when he says that there are few "self-executing" Presidential orders.[1] In point of fact, present-day observers of organizations are now convinced that many factors must converge before rules, orders, edicts, fiats, commands, and the like are obeyed with strict or even substantially close adherence to the manifest intent of the man on top.

Traditional theory also has it that when the Supreme Court sneezes, lesser courts jump. In other words, the traditional theory on constitutional hierarchical relationships was at least as, if not more, rigid than theory on all other organizations. Indeed, this assumption of lower court lock-step compliance still serves as a central pillar for the anachronistic but persistent practice of many political scientists to describe (with loving detail) what the Supreme Court says, i.e., the field of "Constitutional Law"—and stopping there. The assump-

1. Richard Neustadt, *Presidential Power* (New York: Wiley & Sons, 1960).

61

tion remains that what the Court wills has everything to do with subsequent lower court realities despite the fact that modern organizational theories, modern theories on inter-court relations, and a multitude of myth-shattering events of our recent past have raised serious doubts about the validity of this, the most durable of formal organizational theories.

Jack Peltason was the first "new breed" political scientist to go about observing the impact of the Supreme Court's decision on lower courts. In 1954 he had this to say:

> Defeated by the Supreme Court, the adversely affected interests can regain victory in the lower courts. The Supreme Court normally returns cases to trial judges via the intermediate appellate tribunals. It is these trial judges who have to interpret and apply the Supreme Court decisions, and they can do so in order to minimize the significance of their superior's orders. Between 1941 and 1951 out of 175 cases which the Supreme Court reversed and remanded to state tribunals there were forty-six cases involving further litigation. "In slightly less than half of these cases the party successful in the Supreme Court was unsuccessful in the state court following the remand." Thus even for the immediate parties, a Supreme Court victory is not cause for too much celebration. As between the interests, Supreme Court victory for one hardly means that the other lost the war.[2]

Some time later, Peltason focused his research on the federal judiciary of the South to see their reaction to the school desegregation decisions of the Supreme Court.[3] What he saw prompted him to call the resulting book, most aptly, "Fifty-Eight Lonely Men." [4]

At that time, the Supreme Court ordered that Southern school officials desegregate their educational facilities with "all deliberate speed." It became immediately incumbent on federal judges to determine the reasonableness of a gaggle of integration programs drummed up by Southern officialdom, most of which were designed to coddle age-old segregation practices. Some fourteen years later, published

2. Jack Peltason, The Federal Courts in the Political Process (New York: Doubleday, 1955), p. 60.
3. In particular, of course, Brown v. Board of Education 347 U.S. 483 (1954).
4. Fifty-Eight Lonely Men (N.Y.: Harcourt, Brace & World, 1961). See also, Leon Friedman (ed.), Southern Justice (N.Y.: Pantheon, 1965).

statistics revealed that less than 3 per cent of Southern schools could in any way be classified as desegregated. One wag put it this way: "The Supreme Court got little speed and much deliberation." It was a way of saying what Peltason found out: the Court's mandate was really so vague, and gave the lower court judges so much discretion, that they could make decisions that were far more consistent with their own anti-integration attitudes and the like-minded social and political mores that prevailed in their own local communities than with the Court's highly publicized intentions. In effect, the Court was its own undoing; a man will not bring undue hardship upon himself and his family if he does not have to—even if he is a federal district court judge.

Generally speaking, the ambiguity of the command, the proximity of a subordinate to strong community pressures, and his preferences (personal attitudes) will influence execution. This seems to apply to trial judges as much as it does to the lower-echelon bureaucrat— though there may well be differences as yet unearthed. Peltason also found that as any of these factors might vary, so might the effective application of the Court's mandate. For instance, the Court of Appeals judges, also home-grown products of Southern culture, followed the Supreme Court far more assiduously than did their federal district court counterparts. One reason for this might have been that a circuit court is far better insulated from local pressures; few circuit judges hail from the seat where their court sits. As the influence of local pressures diminishes, it becomes less risky for the lower court judge to defer to the intent expressed in a highly provocative Supreme Court decision.

There have been some other highly insightful works on the impact of a Supreme Court decision on lower court judges. Two of them follow. Walter Murphy's article on "lower court checks" supplements Peltason's work by revealing an even wider variety of available methods by which *federal* judges can resist the Court's manifest desires. Moreover, Murphy describes a plentitude of options open to judges of *state* courts should they disagree also with the Court's constitutional interpretations or policy goals. Kenneth Vines elaborates on how "extra-legal factors" closely relate to highly disparate lower court decisions that are applying (supposedly) the same law (the Supreme Court decision). His work offers statistical support for

Peltason's thesis and covers all aspects of race relations, not simply that of school integration.

Thus, the Murphy and Vines articles embellish the modern theme that attitudes and strategies are as equally operant at lower court levels as they are in the Supreme Court itself. They present an intricate elaboration of how the Supreme Court cannot be said to control the lower courts and, indeed, the impact of the Supreme Court decision on lower courts now appears as intriguingly varied as it is on the other governmental agencies. These essays illustrate why traditional court-hierarchy theory must look increasingly shopworn even to those who have treasured it most dearly.

WALTER F. MURPHY

Lower Court Checks on Supreme Court Power

Practicing politicians as well as students of politics have long recognized the check on presidential power imposed by the federal administrative machinery. High policy must be interpreted; it can sometimes be changed or even frustrated by the bureaucrats who apply laws and executive orders. Officials down the line have interests, loyalties, and ambitions which go beyond and often clash with the allegiance accorded a given tenant of the White House. Each bureaucrat has his own ideas about proper public policy, particularly in his field of special competence. If a career civil servant, he may identify only partially, if at all, the good of the governmental service, not to say the good of the public, with the ends sought by the Administration. And if he owes his appointment or promotion to other sources than the merit system, he may find a positive conflict between his loyalties to the President and to other politicians or political groups.

This conflict can occur at all administrative levels. Cabinet members may make up the President's official family, but some of them are at times his chief rivals for power within his own political party, or, more often, representatives of those rivals. Or the department heads may be so split with sibling political rivalry among themselves that common loyalty to their nominal leader may be subordinated to other values. An observer has lately written: "The conditions which a system of fragmented power sets for the success and the survival of a Cabinet officer encourage him to consolidate his own nexus of

From *The American Political Science Review*, 53 (Dec. 1959), pp. 1017–31. Reprinted by permission of the publisher and the author.

Walter F. Murphy is Professor of Politics at Princeton University and has been Chairman of the Department of Politics at Princeton since 1966.

power and compel him to operate with a degree of independence from the President." [1]

Internal friction or drag is is thus an inherent part of the executive process, a factor to be weighed in choosing among policy alternatives, much the same as congressional, or judicial, or pressure group resistance. Less obviously, but not necessarily less significantly, a similar bureaucratic factor must be reckoned with in the execution of Supreme Court decisions. Except in disputes between states or the rare litigation involving diplomats, the Supreme Court usually does not render either the initial or the final decision in a case. If it reverses a state decision, the Court remands the case to state courts for disposition "not inconsistent with this opinion"; and it frequently gives only slightly more precise directions in overruling federal tribunals. The Supreme Court typically formulates general policy. Lower courts apply that policy, and working in its interstices, inferior judges may materially modify the High Court's determinations.

I

As might be expected, state judges have a wider field in which to operate. Two technical rules help to enlarge their area of discretion. The first, already mentioned, is the vague criteria which the Supreme Court imposes when it overturns a state decision. Second, the Supreme Court will review only those state cases which were based on a substantial federal question. The Court has reiterated time and again its practice of not reviewing state decisions which have sufficient independent grounding in state law so that a reversal of the determinations of federal issues would not affect the final outcome of the case. . . .

Considering the perennial friction between state and national interests and outlooks, the different elements weighed in the appointment of state and federal judges, their allegiances (former if not current) to opposing political parties or to separate levels of party

1. Richard F. Fenno, Jr., "President-Cabinet Relations: A Pattern and a Case Study," *American Political Science Review* 52 (1958), pp. 388, 404. (Italics in original omitted.)

hierarchy, the different ambitions of the judges, and their varying conceptions of the role of the judiciary in a federal and democratic system, the wonder is that occasions of open conflict are the exception rather than the rule. Perhaps the use of the vague remand prescription acts as a psychological safety valve in allowing some of the pressure of resentment against reversal to be siphoned off in construing Supreme Court instructions.[2]

An additional safety valve is criticism of Supreme Court decisions, a practice in which judges who have been reversed engage only slightly less bitterly than disappointed litigants. The most serious recent verbal attack came when the 1958 Conference of State Chief Justices issued a sharp accusation that Justices of the Supreme Court were usurping state judicial power by confusing their own policy views with constitutional commands.[3] The Conference chose to launch this attack at the strategic moment when congressional assaults against the Supreme Court had reached a climax.

Both these devices permit exercise of power as well as escape of pressure. Criticism may persuade the Court of the error of its ways, or help convince Congress of a need for remedial legislation. The interpreting authority may even be stretched to accomplish a *de facto* overturning of Supreme Court decisions. A study published in 1954 reported that in eleven terms, some 46 Supreme Court reversals of state decisions required additional litigation. "In slightly less than half of these cases the party successful in the Supreme Court was unsuccessful in the state court following the remand."[4] This study also indicated that, with one exception,[5] the evasion had been accomplished by interpretation rather than by defiance. For example, when the High Court ruled in 1952 that Oklahoma's loyalty oath violated due process in not distinguishing between knowing and innocent

2. For historical accounts of state court defiance of Supreme Court decisions, see Charles Warren, "Federal and State Court Interference," *Harvard L. Rev.*, Vol. 43, p. 345 (1930); and Note, "Interposition v. Judicial Power," *Race Rel. L. Rep.*, Vol. 1, p. 465 (1956).
3. *Resolutions Adopted at the Tenth Annual Meeting of the Conference of Chief Justices* (Chicago: Council of State Governments, mimeo., 1958).
4. Note, "Congressional Reversal of Supreme Court Decisions, 1945–57," *Harvard L. Rev.* 73 (1958), p. 1324.
5. Ashcraft v. Tennessee, 322 U.S. 143 (1944); 327 U.S. 274 (1946). The intervening Tennessee decisions are unreported.

membership in proscribed organizations,[6] the Oklahoma court in which the case had begun read *scienter* into the state statute and sustained the judicially amended version.[7]

The line between evasion and defiance is always difficult to draw, and when in 1954 the Supreme Court declared Jim Crow legally dead,[8] the attitude of many segregationist state judges shifted perceptibly. Yet the manner in which Southern judicial resistance has been expressed is significant. These judges have criticized the *School Segregation* decisions on and off the bench; they were among the leaders of the movement in the 1958 Conference of State Chief Justices to reprimand the Supreme Court. They have given moral support and, one may guess, perhaps legal advice to Southern political leaders. But when pressed, no state supreme court has yet failed to concede that the School Segregation cases are the law of the land and binding on lower courts. Resistance of state supreme courts (and, though not universally, of state lower courts) has taken three specific forms: (1) refusing to expand the school decision to other areas; (2) upholding the constitutionality of state efforts to evade compliance; and (3), in line with the state chief justices' censure, balking at Supreme Court decisions in related areas of race and of federal-state relations.

*   *   *

II

There are both similarities and differences between the political relations of state courts and lower federal courts to the Supreme Court. Formal state-federal competition is absent, but it is often replaced by a local-national clash which can be almost equally as abrasive. This, in turn, is affected by the varying considerations in appointment of lower and Supreme Court judges. The Executive Department chooses district and, to a lesser extent, circuit judges in close cooperation with senators and national committeemen from the

6. Wieman v. Updegraff, 344 U.S. 183 (1952).
7. The lower court decision is unreported. The details can be found in the follow-up case of the same title, 301 P. 2d 1003 (Sup. Ct. of Okla., 1956).
8. Brown v. Board, 347 U.S. 483 (1954); 349 U.S. 294 (1955).

President's party and occasionally with congressmen from the state or states involved. Even a senator from the opposition party may enter the bargaining process. It would not be much of an exaggeration to say, as President Taft once did, that at least as regards district judges, the President's power is largely one of veto rather than of full scale appointment.[9]

At the Supreme Court level there are still many political restrictions on the appointing power, but the President can weigh these competing values on a national rather than on a local scale. Even if Eisenhower's judicial probation-promotion policy remains in effect, High Court members are likely to be different types of men from those usually selected for the lower bench.

When the normal friction between trial and appellate judge is added to these other factors, a substantial reservoir of potential conflict has been built up. On the other hand, several forces act to soften this strife. First, and this bond unites federal with state judges as well as the three levels of federal judges with each other, they are all participants in the cult of the robe. They share the same holy mysteries and dispense the same sacred doctrine. No matter how fierce their inter-court rivalries, common possession of this magic sets judges apart from the rest of men and gives them interests and outlooks as *judges*. Second, district, circuit, and Supreme Court judges are all *federal* officials, in a sense joint competitors, whether they like it or not, with state judges for power.

The concept of an independent judiciary, which can increase the number of collisions between state and national tribunals, is balanced within the national system by appellate court supervision which, if it does not prevent conflict, does help keep that conflict from coming out into the open. A state judge owes his appointment to local political groups and can be removed, if at all, only by state action. Federal district and circuit judges are made even more independent by their life tenure, but their inferior position in the hierarchical chain of national authority subjects them to more strict Supreme Court surveillance. Under its power as supervisor of the administration of federal justice, the Supreme Court can set more exacting standards for lower courts of the United States than for state tribunals.

9. Quoted in George H. Haynes, *The Senate of the United States: Its History and Practice* (Boston, 1938), II, 722.

This makes federal court defiance less likely than state, but district and circuit judges are not mere pawns in the judicial game. They sometimes lash out in caustic criticism too. In 1958, for example, the Court of Appeals for the Ninth Circuit reversed the conviction of a pair of communist leaders on the basis of the Supreme Court's narrow interpretations of the Smith Act in *Yates v. United States*.[10] Judge Chambers remarked tartly that the court would have upheld the validity of the convictions on the basis of past practice had not the Supreme Court changed the law. "One may as well recognize that the Yates decision leaves the Smith Act, as to any further prosecutions under it, a virtual shambles—unless the American Communist Party should witlessly set out to reconstitute itself again with a new 'organization'." [11]

The reactions of a number of lower federal judges to the state chief justices' censure of the Supreme Court were no more subtle. The *U. S. News and World Report* polled all district and circuit judges, asking if they agreed or disagreed with the report of the state chief justices. Only 128 of 351 answered: 59 of them expressed approval, 50 disapproval, and 19 voiced no opinion.[12]

Another channel of criticism, more discreet but also more directly pointed toward securing remedial congressional action, is the Judicial Conference,[13] either at the national or circuit level. The Judicial Conference of the United States several times in recent years has endorsed bills to reverse Supreme Court decisions allowing relatively liberal opportunities for state prisoners to seek *habeas corpus* in federal courts.[14] But it was the Judicial Conference for the District of Columbia Circuit which struck one of the harshest blows with this weapon.

At the close of its 1956 term the Supreme Court had, in *Mallory*

10. 354 U.S. 298 (1957).
11. Fujimoto v. United States, 251 F. 2d 342, 342 (1958). The other two circuit judges specifically disassociated themselves from these comments on the Yates case.
12. October 24, 1958, pp. 36–37.
13. 28 U.S.C. §331 provides that every year the Chief Justice of the United States shall call a meeting of the chief judges of each circuit, the chief judge of the Court of Claims, and a district judge from each circuit. . . .
14. *Annual Report of the Proceedings of the Judicial Conference of the United States* (Washington, 1958), p. 28. Earlier recommendations are summarized in *House Report No. 1293 on H.R. 8361*, 85th Cong., 2d Sess. . . .

v. *United States*,[15] extended the application of its libertarian decision in the earlier *McNabb* case.[16] *McNabb* had ruled that confessions secured as a result of questioning during a prolonged period of delay between arrest and arraignment could not be used as evidence in a federal court. While the delay in *McNabb* had been several days, in *Mallory* less than eight hours had elapsed between arrest and confession. Nevertheless, the Court held that even this shorter period fell within the prohibition against "unnecessary delay" in arraignment imposed by Rule 5(a) of the Federal Rules of Criminal Procedure. Frankfurter's unanimous opinion conceded that "circumstances may justify a brief delay," but the police must "arraign the arrested person as quickly as possible so that he may be advised of his rights and so that the issue of probable cause may be promptly determined." [17] The Federal Rules were declared to allow "arresting officers little more leeway than the interval between arrest and the ordinary administrative steps required to bring a suspect before the nearest available magistrate." [18]

This decision, resulting as it did in the freeing of a chronic criminal who had just been found guilty of a brutal rape, stirred up a hornet's nest in Congress [19] as well as more tactfully expressed displeasure among lower court judges. At its next meeting, the Judicial Conference for the District of Columbia Circuit, the circuit in which *Mallory* had originated, endorsed pending legislation which would have rewritten Rule 5(a) so as to erase the *McNabb-Mallory* holdings.[20]

* * *

The Supreme Court had spoken in *Mallory*, and while its opinion obviously did not set precise or very narrow limitations on lower

15. 354 U.S. 449 (1957).
16. 318 U.S. 332 (1943).
17. 354 U.S. 449, 454 (1957).
18. *Ibid.*, at 453.
19. A number of bills to reverse the Mallory decision were introduced in the 85th Congress. H.R. 11477 passed both the House and Senate, but in somewhat different forms. The conference report was agreed to by the House, but was defeated in the Senate minutes before final adjournment when Senator Carroll (D., Colo.) raised a point of order which Vice President Nixon sustained.
20. *Washington Post & Times Herald*, May 9, 1958.

The authority to make findings of fact gives trial judges extensive power which appellate tribunals can only partially control.[28] And in the *School Segregation Cases,* the Supreme Court broadened the scope of this inherent authority by specifically directing the exercise of the widest sort of judicial discretion, guided only by the flexible formula "with all deliberate speed." This is obviously a grant of vast power, and the high bench has relied on the Courts of Appeals to supervise its exercise. At this writing, after four years of lower court administration of school segregation problems, the Supreme Court has consented to full-scale review of only one such decision,[29] and there it affirmed the Court of Appeals.

Such a policy constitutes a manifestation of faith as well as an invitation for assumption of power. And occasionally a judge will seize the full implications of this invitation. Flying directly in the face of the desegregation ruling, and even after one reversal by the Court of Appeals, District Judge William H. Atwell declined to order Dallas, Texas, to set a date for integration because this would cause "civil wrongs." Lest his own feelings be mistaken, Atwell declared: "I believe that it will be seen that the [Supreme] Court based its decision on no law but rather on what the Court regarded as more authoritative, modern psychological knowledge. . . . It will be recalled that in 1952, Mr. Justice Frankfurter said it was not competent to take judicial notice of Claims of social scientists.' "[30]

As a retired jurist called back for temporary service, Judge Atwell may have felt a wider margin of freedom than his more active brethren, but the significant fact remains that 48 months after the Supreme Court's implementation decision neither of the two Southern communities in which the original school cases began had yet been required to admit a single Negro child to a hitherto white school.[31] Indeed, although there had been several court orders for a

28. See especially Jerome Frank, *Courts on Trial: Myth and Reality in American Justice* (Princeton: Princeton University Press, 1950). . . .
29. Cooper v. Aaron, 3 L. ed. 2d 5 (1958).
30. Bell v. Rippy, 146 F. Supp. 485, 486 (1956). The earlier decision is reported at 133 F. Supp. 811 (1955), and the reversal, *sub nom.* . . .
31. In the case which originated in Prince Edward County, Virginia, the district judge in 1958 set 1965 as the date for compliance, 164 F. Supp. 786 (1958). The Court of Appeals reversed, and ordered admission of qualified Negro students to hitherto white schools in September 1959, 266 F. 2d 507 (1959). The county replied in June, 1959 by refusing to appropriate money for continued operation of public schools. . . .

"prompt start" on plans for eventual segregation, when the school year closed in June, 1959, the only two Deep Southern states to have even token public school integration in some localities were North Carolina and Virginia.

This is not to deny that most federal judges are trying their best to carry out desegregation in a sincere and workable manner, but even the most imaginative member of the realist school of jurisprudence could hardly conceive of a more fertile field for free play of judicial predilections, conscious and sub-conscious. As a reaction against this freedom and its resultant responsibility, there is evidence of a growing resentment among lower court judges in Southern and border states, a feeling that they have been left to engage in a violent emotional battle against prevailing white mores while the Justices in Washington refuse to stoop to such conflict by primly denying certiorari in segregation cases.

It is possible that the Court of Appeals for the Eighth Circuit in the August 1958 phase of the Little Rock campaign was trying to force the Supreme Court's hand when it took the somewhat unusual step of staying its own order to preserve the *status quo*.[32] If the case had not been immediately reviewed by the Supreme Court, the stay would have allowed Central High School to transfer its Negro students and to reopen as a segregated institution. This would have been an immense victory for Governor Faubus's obstructionist tactics.

If the Court of Appeals was trying to compel the High Bench to reiterate its principles and re-enter the fight, the circuit judges succeeded wonderfully well. Both the opinion of the Chief Justice and Frankfurter's concurrence spelled out the Court's constitutional authority and interpretation, as well as its policy intentions, in a far more powerful form than had either of the two previous school decisions.[33]

32. Cooper v. Aaron, 257 F. 2d 33 (1958).
33. Cooper v. Aaron, 3 L. ed. 2d 5 (1958).

KENNETH N. VINES

Federal District Judges and Race Relations Cases in the South

Among those nations with federal arrangements of political power, the United States is one of the few maintaining a national judiciary through the states.[1] Unlike other federal systems where federal judges adjudicate only at the appellate level, United States district judges have a large and continuing area of original jurisdiction. They decide thousands of cases each year and hold court in every state in the union.

The widespread location of a federal judicial power has important consequences for the operation of the American political process. In the first place, an important institution embodying national power is added to the political process at the state level. District courts initiate policy, they implement or may overrule policy made elsewhere in the political system. Further, political interests and factions in the several states may make political demands upon the federal courts as well as on federal legislators and administrators and all members of the state political system. Estimating their probable success, interested parties may choose to make claims in the first instance before the federal courts, or they may turn there as a last resort if efforts elsewhere in the political system have been unsuccessful.

* * *

1. Two others are Argentina and Mexico. Wiencyzslaw Wagner, *The Federal States and Their Judiciary* (Mouton and Co., 1959), pp. 165–72.

From the *Journal of Politics*, 26: 2 (May 1964), pp. 337–57. Reprinted by permission of the publisher and the author.

Kenneth N. Vines is a Professor of Political Science at the State University of New York (SUNY) at Buffalo.

An excellent opportunity to study the district courts may be found in the quantity of race relations cases which have occurred in recent years in the U.S. district courts in the South. Collectively, the cases involve important judicial policy making in the district courts. Cases concerning race relations have occurred in all eleven of the traditional states of the South, and, in varying quantities, in every judicial district.

The purpose of this paper is to explore the political activities of officials operating within a judicial environment, in a sensitive, crucial area of Southern politics. This will be done by an examination of race relations cases in Southern federal district courts. The disposition of cases will be described and the distribution of decisions related to judicial districts and to deciding judges. Finally, an attempt will be made to explain the similarities and differences in the decisions. The cases examined will include all race relations cases decided in the federal district courts of the eleven states of the traditional South from May 1954 to October 1962. Data concerning the disposition of these cases will be used in conjunction with information on the backgrounds and experiences of Southern district judges and with certain information on the judicial districts in which the cases were decided.

Political scientists have shown that a variety of political institutions are molded by their economic and social environment and that political behavior is related to the social backgrounds and political experiences of the participants. Legal theory supposes, however, that courts and judges, because of the myth of legal objectivity and the quasi-insulated position of the courts from the remainder of the political system, are not similarly influenced, except perhaps by their legal environment. Judicial analysts have frequently shown that judges do vary in their behavior but have not often attempted to explain the variations in judicial behavior. Through investigation of a homogeneous group of cases decided by judges in the context of a region with both social similarities and social differences, we have an opportunity to examine the behavior of judges against their social and political environment. Then we may see whether judges and courts are also molded by their social and political environment or whether legal theory correctly describes judicial behavior.

*   *   *

DISTRIBUTION OF CASES

The amount of race relations policy conflict settled in the Southern
federal district courts is shown in Table 1. Most of the 291 [2] cases
represent policy demands initiated by Negroes and offer proof that
the federal judiciary has become an important arena for the handling
of Negro claims in the political system, at the local and regional
levels. During the same period of time we have evidence that other
institutions in the state and regional political process handled few
Negro claims.[3] The race relations cases in the Southern district courts
highlight the possibility of access to the courts when other points in
the political process are closed or unfavorable. Nor is this necessarily
due to more favorable attitudes on the part of the district judges.
Because claims are presented to courts according to fixed procedures
and under stated and known jurisdictional criteria, cases can be heard
irrespective of the attitudes of the judge.

Table 1 also describes the distribution of cases by period and
subject matter. Cases on education were by far the most numerous
type and accounted for more than half the total work of the courts
during this period. . . .

As Table 2 indicates, Negroes, in spite of their reputation for
success in the federal courts, won decisions in barely more than half
(51.3 per cent) of all cases. Decisions in favor of Negroes varied,
however, in different subject categories and during different periods.
Only where the cases concerned education have Negroes won more
than half the cases litigated before the Southern federal bar. Where
agencies of the federal government have pushed and where higher
court precedents are prominent, as in those cases involving voting,
transportation, and desegregation of government facilities, Negro
success is measured at or near the fifty per cent mark, indicating the

2. For a descriptive treatment of some of the more important cases on desegregation, see J. W. Peltason, *Fifty-Eight Lonely Men* (Harcourt, Brace and
World, 1961), and Robert Steamer, "The Role of the Federal District Courts
in the Segregation Controversy," *Journal of Politics*, Vol. 22, pp. 417–38.
3. Cases concerned with remand and vacate orders are not included since,
legally, these are directives to proceed and not genuine policy decisions although in practice remand orders are sometimes not followed by the district
courts.

Table 1

DISTRIBUTION OF RACE RELATIONS DECISIONS IN SOUTHERN DISTRICT
COURTS BY SUBJECT AND PERIOD (N=291)

Subject	Percentage of Total Cases
Education	52.7
Government facilities	16.0
Voting	11.3
Transportation	8.3
Trial procedures	3.3
Employment	2.2
Other (other civil rights, criminal law, defense of Negro organizations)	6.2
	100.0
Period	
I – May 1954–1957 (43 months)	22.2
II – 1958–1960 (36 months)	38.9
III – 1961–Oct. 1962 (22 months)	38.9
	100.0

*   *   *

Table 2

PERCENTAGE OF RACE RELATIONS CASES FAVORING NEGROES BY SUBJECT
AND PERIOD OF DECISION (N=291)

Subject	Percentage Favoring Negroes
Education	60.7
Government facilities	47.7
Voting	48.4
Transportation	47.8
Trial procedures	11.1
Employment	16.7
Other	23.5
All cases	51.3
Period	
I – May 1954–1957	52.4
II – 1958–1960	44.9
III – 1961–Oct. 1962	57.0

influence of the legal environment. But in other areas not so well
marked by precedent or government intervention, such as employment, defense of Negro organizations, and other civil rights, Negro
interests have been much less successful in the adjudication of favorable policies.

The differential success of Negroes in different types of cases also
suggests that more than the mere following of precedents from higher
courts is involved. The directives from the Supreme Court in favor
of Negro groups on the subject of transportation and voting are
clearer than those on education; but the activities of opposing interest
groups have been more energetic and inventive in the field of voting
and especially in education. Yet the federal district courts have
decided much more frequently in favor of Negro litigants in the
field of education than in either of the two fields cited above. Apparently precedent alone, even from the U.S. Supreme Court, does not
dictate the direction of the disposition of cases in the district courts.

The success of Negro interests seems related to the amount of
litigation.

*   *   *

THE DISTRICTS

*   *   *

Federal district judges commonly come from the district which they
serve. . . . Their ties with the judicial district in which they serve
are consequently deep and of long standing. Moreover, while in
office, judges are required by statute to continue living in the district
of appointment.[4]

*   *   *

Because of the location of the courts in scattered districts Frankfurter and Landis regard localism, or the influence of those factors of
the local environment, as a key characteristic of the federal district

4. *United States Code*, 28:134, 1958.

court system, the root conception of its organization.[5] And while they interpret localism essentially in organizational and administrative terms, it is clearly a factor in political behavior as well. Some political scientists suggest that local influences have a decisive impact on policy makers who represent and are elected from districts. In a sense federal judges represent the district to which they are appointed. They must live in the district, usually sit only in that district, and hear all the cases of proper jurisdiction occurring in the district. Demands for policy enactment which are judicable must be made before the constituents' district court, just as requests are made of one's district Congressman.

*   *   *

. . . A number of studies have indicated that a large percentage of Negroes in the population affects in an important way the policy processes in the South. In general those parts of the South with the least proportion of Negroes in the population have been most permissive in attitudes towards race relations while those sections with a large proportion have been less tolerant. One study which investigated the influence of a number of factors in the Southern environment on Negro registration levels found that Negro-white population balance was the most significant of all factors in affecting Southern policy.[6] Southern judicial districts differ widely among themselves with respect to the presence of this important factor, ranging from a low of 4.1 per cent in the East Tennessee district to a high of 51.1 per cent in the South Alabama district.

*   *   *

There is considerable variation in the way different judicial districts disposed of race relations cases, as described by Table 3. In dealing with similar political problems often stated in similar legal ways, Southern district courts evidenced quite wide differences in

5. Felix Frankfurter and James Landis, *The Business of the Supreme Court* (Macmillan and Co., 1927), pp. 218–19.
6. Donald Matthews and James Prothro, "State Political Systems and Negro Voter Registration in the South," unpublished article, p. 16.

their decisions. Given the differences among the districts in Negro-white population balance, we can find whether or not the two variables are related. A measure of relationship would provide one test of the proposition that courts are influenced by their social environment.

Table 3
DISPOSITION OF CASES BY JUDICIAL DISTRICTS

Percentage Favoring Negroes	Number of Districts
90–100	3
80–89	2
70–79	1
60–69	5
50–59	5
40–49	2
30–39	3
20–29	2
10–19	0
Below 10	5
	28

The coefficient of correlation between the two factors is $R = -48$. That is, the proportion of Negroes in the population of Southern judicial districts is negatively related to the percentage of cases decided in favor of Negroes in the district. The higher the proportion of Negroes in a district, the less apt, at least to the extent of $R = -48$, is the court to decide the cases in favor of Negroes.

*   *   *

THE DISTRICT JUDGES—INFLUENTIAL FACTORS

Among the 60 judges who sat in the Southern district courts on race relations cases from 1954–1962 there were . . . 37 judges who sat on 3 or more cases and among them these judges decided 267 cases. . . .

*   *   *

Ranked according to the disposition of cases for and against Negroes, the judges fall into three groups: the first group we may call the "Segregationists" and they decided in favor of Negroes in less than one-third of the cases; the second group who decided in favor of Negroes in 34–67 per cent of all cases handled, we call the "Moderates"; the third group whose record in favor of Negro claimants was better than 67 per cent of all cases, we call the "Integrationists." These terms are doubtless not an accurate description of the judicial philosophies of the respective groups, but they can serve as identifications for the three groups and as rough indicators of their roles in Southern politics.

* * *

The factor of Negro-white population balance, we have seen, has limited explanatory power in accounting for the differences in the disposition of cases within the various districts. For further information on the factors associated with the differential judicial behavior, we may turn to the judges themselves, their backgrounds and experiences. Some studies of judicial behavior in various courts have indicated that judicial behavior is related to the social backgrounds and political experiences of the judges.[7] The general thesis in all these studies is that social and political factors are related to judicial behavior in much the same fashion that social and political characteristics are related to the political behavior of voters and non-judicial policy makers.

* * *

. . . Historically, the Democratic party in the South has been identified with the maintenance of segregation and white supremacy, while the Southern Republican party has a tradition of a more permissive attitude in race relations. Consequently, we might wonder whether judicial behavior in the South is related to partisan affiliation.

7. See my "Political Functions of a State Supreme Court," *Tulane Studies in Political Science*, Vol. 8, pp. 51–75; and John Schmidhauser, "Judicial Behavior and the Sectional Crisis of 1837–1860," *Journal of Politics*, Vol. 23 (1961), pp. 615–641.

Table 4
PARTY AFFILIATIONS OF THREE GROUPS OF SOUTHERN JUDGES *

Affiliation	Segregationists	Moderates	Integrationists
Democratic	78.6%	50.0%	45.4
Republican	21.4	50.0	54.6
	100.0 (N = 14)	100.0 (N = 12)	100.0 (N = 11)

* X^2 indicates marginal significance at .08 level.

The figures in Table 4 indicate that the Republican judges are located disproportionately among the Moderates and Integrationists, half of whose members are Republicans. Only 3 out of 14, or 21.4 per cent, of the Segregationist judges are Republicans. Republican candidates in the South today are often as enthusiastically in favor of segregation and as racially demagogic as their Democratic opponents. Yet, there is some evidence here that the traditions of the Southern Republican party still have some impact upon political behavior. The relative isolation of Southern Republicans may also contribute to their more permissive attitude toward Negroes in race relations cases. Even if active and politically involved, Southern Republicans are apt to have fewer occasions to seek state political office, to attend regional political meetings, and publicly to defend Southern political values. The political roles which result in white supremacy among the Democratic office seekers and party workers are often lacking in the more restricted political lives of Southern Republicans. A further possible explanation may be found in the character of the Republican judges appointed by Eisenhower. Not restricted by senatorial courtesy, the President was able to appoint with relative freedom and his appointments include the "new" Republicans with urban backgrounds.

*   *   *

Religious affiliation, while it cannot be considered of great significance in itself, may provide a clue to the relationship of the judge to the Southern social structure. Very largely (except in quite restricted areas such as Southern Louisiana) Southern society is Protestant and orthodox. The Protestant church far from providing an exception to the structure of a segregated society, remains an almost totally segregated institution and must be regarded as one of the important institutional supports of traditional Southern values.

Table 5

RELIGIOUS AFFILIATION OF GROUPS OF SOUTHERN JUDGES *

Religious Affiliation	Segregationists	Moderates	Integrationists
Orthodox Protestant	71.4%	66.7%	36.4%
Catholic	0.0	0.0	18.2
None listed	21.4	25.0	45.4
Don't know	7.2	8.3	0.0
	100.0% (N = 14)	100.0% (N = 12)	100.0% (N = 11)

* X² indicates significance at .05 level.

The data in Table 5 indicate that there are significant differences among the groups of judges on the matter of religious affiliation. Only about one-third of the Integrationists list orthodox Protestant religions (36.4 per cent) while two-thirds or more of the Moderates (66.7 per cent) and the Segregationists (71.4 per cent) list such religion. The few Catholic judges are found among the Integrationists and almost half of the Integrationists (45.4 per cent) list no religion. We may speculate that the non-affiliation of the Integrationists with orthodox Protestant religions provides suggestive evidence that these judges are not closely related to the conventional social structure; this may be one of the sources of their unorthodox conduct of race relations cases.

The path to the district judiciary in the South, as Table 6 shows, has often involved holding public office. Experience in public office has been important in the careers of judges in all three groups, but there are some important differences in the types of experiences. No office, federal or state, judicial or non-judicial, has dominated the political experiences of all three groups with uniform frequency. While close to one-half of the Segregationists (57.1 per cent) and the Moderates (41.1 per cent) have held state office, only 9.1 per cent of the Integrationists have. Federal offices have been occupied by nearly half the Segregationists (42.9 per cent) and the Integrationists (45.5 per cent) but by only 8.4 per cent of the Moderates.

Table 6 *

PREVIOUS PUBLIC OFFICES HELD BY SOUTHERN JUDGES **

Public Office	Segregationists (N = 14)	Moderates (N = 12)	Integrationists (N = 11)
State political office	57.1%	41.7%	9.1%
Federal political office	42.9	8.4	45.5
State judicial office	50.0	33.3	9.1
Federal judicial office	28.6	8.4	45.5
State and local judgeship	35.7	33.3	0.0

* Columns do not add up to 100.0 per cent because some judges held more than one office.
** X² indicates significance at .01 level.

Looking at the variation in the types of offices held by the three groups we may advance some suggestions concerning the relationship between political experience on the way to the bench and judicial behavior. Since about half of both the Segregationists and the Integrationists held federal office before coming to the court, we may conclude that political experiences gained in the services of the federal government do not function as an educational experience for the judge steeped in the values of Southern society. As a district attorney or assistant district attorney, the judicial candidate prosecutes cases involving various national political values, meets numerous kinds of litigants and serves in many political situations. Such experiences might be expected to broaden the outlook of prospective judges inducing respect for national values when these conflict with regional ones. However, federal political experience is apparently not enough, by itself, to accomplish this.

Tenure in a state political position, on the other hand, could strengthen the identification of the judge with Southern norms. As a legislator, state administrator, or state judge, he is often called upon to enact or enforce policies which implement the Southern point of view and sometimes to defend these values against what is called federal encroachment. Moreover, in seeking office, regional symbols may be invoked, or at least, paid lip service. The difference between Segregationist and Integrationist judges here is striking. Well over half the Segregationists (57.1 per cent) have held state political office while only 9.1 per cent of the Integrationists or less than one-tenth have held state office.

The Segregationist group is clearly distinguished from the Integrationist group by pre-judicial experiences in state government. Both in policy making and campaigning the Southern state officeholder can rarely remain indifferent to the issues involving the political and social position of the Negro. The frequency with which Segregationist judges have held state office suggests that state political experience corroborates Southern values. Integrationists, on the other hand, have seldom held state political positions. When they have held public office, it has been a federal one and in all cases also a federal judicial office. Here the service of judicial candidates as federal attorneys, when not combined with officeholding in the state political structure, seems to have marked out many members of the Integrationist group for deviation from traditional Southern values. It is important that the future judge has not undergone commitment to the state political system. Not identified with the state political system the judge may be more sympathetic toward national values and less sympathetic toward Southern state efforts to resist federal policies.

*   *   *

The evidence points to the conclusion that Southern federal judges in district courts are influenced by their social and political environment. In this they join other Southern politicians, state legislators, Congressmen, and state executives, who also respond to local factors. To this extent, we can say that judges, though ostensibly "different," react to environmental factors like other policy makers. We do not exclude the possibility of the influence of the legal environment upon the behavior of judges, but suggest that if legalistic influences are operative they must be considered along with social and political factors.

3 Impact on State and Local Government and Politics

In the past decade or so, the Supreme Court of the United States has rendered several decisions that, if fully implemented, would have wrought drastic modifications in American life. The target of these decisions was state and local officialdom and the message was that it should mend its ways. To the Supreme Court, law was being violated —and flagrantly; that is, many officials of state and local government were acting unconstitutionally with full knowledge of that fact. They were told to refrain from certain activities and to adopt new policies or methods of procedure. Some of these Supreme Court decisions have had penetrating, lasting, broad-gauge effects; some have already had spotty results; and some remain little more than words in a law book. A number of local officials have heard the Court speak and have complied diligently. Others have not bothered to listen. The visible pattern of compliance, evasion, and defiance is highly erratic.

The greatest amount of trickery and stubbornness at the grass roots in response to the Court's wishes has been triggered by the decisions requiring desegregation of educational facilities.[1] Researchers have made it their business to describe the panorama of village, town, city, county, and state reactions to the school desegregation decisions, but perhaps the finest cataloguing of the fruit of Southern ingenuity in

1. The most celebrated one, of course, is *Brown v. Board of Education* 347 U.S. 483 (1954).

89

outflanking the Court is one chapter in a book called *Desegregation and the Law*.[2] I have included portions of that in this section; the title of the chapter is—sadly—"Avoidance, Evasion and Delay."

Meanwhile, researchers have also tried their hand in describing and analyzing the local consequences of other Supreme Court decisions. One area of unusual magnetism for political scientists has been the Court's recent attempt to clarify the law on church-state relations. The Supreme Court has, in a long line of decisions, both validated and forbade special religious programs (e.g., validated some forms of released time for religious education and invalidated others; forbade official prayers, forbade Bible reading) in local public schools.[3] Where the Court legally damned a particular procedure, town reaction was for the most part hostile, for the "nine old men" were attacking God! Lawfully appointed men who considered themselves law-abiding citizens felt little compunction in openly flaunting a Supreme Court decision with which they disagreed morally. Ironically, the supreme law-maker of the land was breeding a new strain of outlaw. Actually, though, this account unfairly accentuates the negative and eliminates the positive, for there has been a good deal of obedience as well. This brings us to the main question: What factors, or factor, are chiefly responsible for whether a local school district rejects, avoids, or accepts the mandate of a Supreme Court decision?

Some modern political scientists have gone beyond mere speculation on this subject and have developed and applied skillful research designs. I have selected several studies to illustrate some of the techniques employed as well as the general run of theories tested. The reader will notice that in this work there is a heavy reliance on questionnaires, sociological data, interviews, and statistical analysis. The studies by Robert Birkby and by Richard Johnson are sophisticated

2. Albert Blaustein and Clarence Ferguson, *Desegregation and the Law* (New Brunswick: Rutgers University Press, 1957). A far more exhaustive listing, though, can be found in Robert B. McKay, "'With All Deliberate Speed': A Study of School Desegregation," *New York University Law Review* 31 (June 1956), pp. 991–1090.
3. See, *McCollum v. Board of Education* 333 U.S. 203 (1948); *Zorach v. Clauson* 343 U.S. 306 (1950); *Engel v. Vitale* 370 U.S. 421 (1962); *Abington School District v. Schempp* 374 U.S. 203 (1963).

successors to Frank Sorauf's trail-blazing survey of released time decisions.[4]

Birkby was interested in locating which factors, if any, linked with 121 Tennessee school district decisions either to notice or ignore the Court mandate against Bible reading. After tracing the pattern of impact, he tested to determine if any relationship existed with such standard factors as: urbanization, extent of religious pluralism in the community, and the socio-economic background of the members of the school board. His findings may astonish the reader. Johnson's research had a more psychological orientation and was confined to an in-depth study of a single Midwestern town.[5] This town, with its close-knit, fundamentalist religious outlook, contrary to what might be expected, abandoned its practice of prayer-reading in the schools in deference to the Court's edict. Johnson undertook to discover why. Armed with a formidable battery of questions, he measured attitudes toward the Court of the superintendent, teachers, principals, the local "influentials," and, of course, the citizenry.

Both studies are extremely valuable for ascertaining the relative importance of several sociological and psychological factors as they may be responsible for the wide variety of reactions at the local level to Court decisions. This is also true of the article by James P. Levine which tries to explain the wide disparity found in twelve states in their implementing of the Supreme Court's definition of "obscenity" in *Roth v. United States*.[6] Of added interest in the Levine piece is his analysis of the tremendous range of opinion represented by the twelve state supreme courts on how to interpret *Roth* or, put another way, how the state courts reconciled the Supreme Court's intent in *Roth* with their own widely divergent prejudices.

A more difficult impact to assess than that of the school decisions is another line of recent Supreme Court opinions on the police and on

4. Frank Sorauf, "*Zorach v. Clauson:* The Impact of a Supreme Court Decision," *American Political Science Review* 53 (Sept. 1959), pp. 777–91. Actually some consider the first judicial impact study in political science to be an offshoot of a dissertation by Gordon Patric. See his "The Impact of a Court Decision: Aftermath of the McCollum Case," *Journal of Public Law* 6 (Fall 1957), pp. 455–64.

5. A fuller account of this study can be found in his: *The Dynamics of Compliance* (Evanston: Northwestern University Press, 1967).

6. *Roth v. United States* 354 U.S. 476 (1957).

law enforcement. The Court, in trying to outline and protect the rights of arrested citizens, has elicited vigorous protests from various police agencies and some legal circles. Also, it has spurred certain political sectors into action. The more popular discussion emphasizes that the police have been severely hampered in their efforts to make arrests, to get confessions and crucial evidence for convictions, and in general to do their job. The thesis of a recent Detroit symposium was: "Has the Supreme Court Handcuffed the Police?" The question could have been worded: "Has the Supreme Court Adequately Increased Citizen Protection Against Overzealous Police?" Issues are framed initially by those who are upset.

In a series of landmark cases, the Court set forth its great dissatisfaction with police procedures of search and seizure and with the treatment of arrestees in the police station.[7] The Court's foremost objective in these cases was to thwart police tactics that brazenly trod upon the rights of citizens. Judges who sit on the Supreme Court find crime waves no more appealing than anyone else, and one can presume that the Justices were sufficiently sensitive to the police contention that their practices were necessary to check criminal behavior. By its decision the Court rejected this argument and said, in effect, that crime rates would not necessarily soar if policemen kept within constitutional bounds. Moreover, we can assume that even if the Justices did believe that there would be an increase in outlawry, they also believed that it would not be so great an evil as to outweigh the degree of harm inherent in continuing (or accelerating) the current degree of abuse of the constitutional rights of Americans by the police themselves. In any event, the decisions were made and several questions as to their impact have been raised: (1) To what extent have the police actually changed their practices? (2) To what extent has any change in police practices affected their ability to make arrests, get important evidence and obtain confessions? (3) To what extent has the crime rate been altered, if at all?

Reliable answers to the first question are hard to come by. One can assume that policemen, like cooks, do not like anyone to peer over their shoulder while they work. Nonetheless, there have been several

7. *Mapp v. Ohio* 367 U.S. 643 (1961); *Escobedo v. Illinois* 378 U.S. 478 (1964); *Miranda v. Arizona* 384 U.S. 436 (1966).

studies that have secured some police co-operation in an attempt to get answers. In addition, there is available probably more objective evidence to help us find answers to the other questions. I am including three studies: one by a group at the Yale Law School (Wald and his associates); one conducted by the Institute for Criminal Law and Procedure at Georgetown Law Center (Medali and his associates); and one by a former Justice of the Michigan Supreme Court (Theodore Sourris). Together they are reasonably representative of the entire run of findings to date on the effects of the Supreme Court decision on American police officers and on the efficacy of law enforcement.[8]

Some observers believe, though, that the most important cases—in terms of actual or potential impact on local (and national) politics —are the famous (or notorious) "one man, one vote" reapportionment decisions.[9] These decisions threatened to thin the ranks of, if not rout, traditionally dominant political coalitions in many state legislatures as well as in Congress. Paul Douglas, speaking as a U.S. Senator, pointed out some of the reasons behind the long-standing malapportionment:

> . . . the legislatures refused to reapportion, partly because the legislators from the overrepresented districts did not want to reapportion, for that would mean that some of the districts would have to be consolidated and the legislators might lose their jobs; but also because the big corporate interests in those States wanted to have the country districts overrepresented because they thought they could control the country districts more than they could con-

8. See also, Jerome Skolnik, *Justice Without Trial* (N.Y.: Wiley and Sons, 1966); Arthur Niederhoffer, *Behind the Shield: The Police in Urban Society* (Garden City, N.Y.: Doubleday, 1967); Nathan Sobel, *The New Confession Standards* (N.Y.: Gould Publication, 1966). Eville Younger, the District Attorney of Los Angeles has also done a study on the impact of Supreme Court decisions on law enforcement and found that it was negligible. See *New York Times*, August 19, 1966.

9. *Reynolds, Judge, et al. v. Sims, et al.* 377 U.S. 533 (1964). Glendon Schubert has amassed an excellent collection of articles and materials on this topic. See his *Reapportionment* (N.Y.: Charles Scribner & Sons, 1965). The case followed the more widely known *Baker v. Carr* 369 U.S. 186 (1962), which opened the whole question of reapportionment to the courts. *Cf.,* Robert G. Dixon, Jr., *Democratic Representation: Reapportionment in Law and Politics* (N.Y.: Oxford University Press, 1968).

trol the urban or city districts in such matters as taxation and utility regulation. That has been one of the forces which has helped to prevent reapportionment.[10]

The most short-range impact of these cases has been the degree to which the state legislatures have been co-operative and done something about existing maldistricting. Naturally, there has been much foot-dragging, but a surprising number acted with dispatch. Thus, in 1965, several years after Senator Douglas's first statement, he could call the following honor roll of reapportioners:

Indiana, in 1963.
Kentucky, in 1963.
Louisiana, for its house, in 1963.
Maryland, very partially-very incompletely, in 1962.
Mississippi, very partially, in 1963.
Nebraska, in 1963.
North Carolina, in 1963, for its senate.
North Dakota, in 1963, for its house.
Pennsylvania, in 1964, for its senate.[11]

The middle-range response is also still in motion. Its most significant aspect is the campaign to restrict the Court decisions on apportionment by changing the Constitution. The spearhead of this drive is the still viable Dirksen amendment. I am including a short essay in this volume from *Congressional Quarterly* which discusses the success of the Dirksen amendment up to 1965 and, additionally, its prospects. Should full or near-full compliance soon come to pass, and the Dirksen counterattack be repulsed, the question of the far-reaching political significance of these decisions will still remain. For instance, what will be the effect of the Supreme Court decisions on the American party system? What consequences will they have for America's peculiar brand of federalism? Martin Landau's article ponders possible answers in the style of the best modern political scientific analysis.

The modern literature on the impact of the Supreme Court decision at the state and local level has added tremendously to our

10. Paul A. Douglas, "Con" in "Controversy over Supreme Court Decisions on Apportionment of State Legislatures," *Congressional Digest* 44 (Jan. 1965), at p. 19.
11. *Ibid.*, p. 19.

knowledge of what happens in State houses and city halls once a decision is announced—and of why it happens. On the other hand, most of these studies have consisted of limited samples and data. Still, though their information is sparse, their findings and speculations are provocative. They demonstrate, most of all, the importance of studying the impact of the Supreme Court decision, that is, to replace soft mythology with hard facts.

ALBERT P. BLAUSTEIN
CLARENCE C. FERGUSON, JR.

Avoidance, Evasion and Delay

Southern opposition to desegregation has led directly to legal measures admittedly designed to circumvent the mandate of *Brown* v. *Board of Education*. But while the avowed purpose of those legal devices is to frustrate the Supreme Court determinations of May 17, 1954, and May 31, 1955, that fact alone does not necessarily make them unconstitutional. Southern lawyers have entered upon a concerted program to find doctrine and precedent which will permit the continued existence of racial segregation and still somehow survive the scrutiny of judicial review. Should they succeed in their quest, those pro-segregation measures which do survive will have met the test of constitutional "legality." Other governmental measures (meaning other governmental actions under color of law) obviously will not survive the requirements of "constitutional" or "legal."

Every legislative enactment, executive order or court decision which conforms to constitutional procedures is a "legal" measure in the sense that it is a manifestation of state action under color of law. And any measure which would be effective in avoiding desegregation would be "legal" in the sense that it had been held valid and binding.

In analyzing the legality of any measure designed to circumvent the operation of an announced rule of law, the courts make an important distinction between "avoidance" and "evasion." There are no

From *Desegregation and the Law* by Albert P. Blaustein and Clarence C. Ferguson, Jr. Copyright © 1957 by Rutgers University Press. Reprinted by permission of the publisher and the author.

Albert P. Blaustein is Professor of Law at Rutgers, The State University. Clarence C. Ferguson, Jr., is Dean of the School of Law at Howard University.

constitutional limitations to measures of "avoidance." It is perfectly proper—at least as far as the courts are concerned—for an individual or a state full of individuals to attempt to "avoid" the consequences of desegregation. "Evasion," on the other hand, is against the law. Individuals who attempt to evade the mandate of *Brown* v. *Board of Education* would be subject to punishment; and governmental measures designed to evade the Supreme Court's conclusions would be struck down as unconstitutional.

Whether an attempt to circumvent a rule of law is "illegal" because it involves "evasion," or whether an attempt at circumvention is labeled "evasion" because it is "illegal" is immaterial. Solution to this problem necessitates an excursion into the realm of legal dialectics which sheds no light on the enforcement problems involved in racial desegregation. The important fact is that circumvention measures in the field of desegregation *may* be "legal," just as they may be "illegal."

An amendment to the Constitution specifically authorizing the states to enact segregation laws would obviously be a legal method of "avoiding" the effects of *Brown* v. *Board of Education*. Legislative re-enactment of the laws which the Supreme Court declared unconstitutional on May 17, 1954, would just as obviously be struck down as an attempt to "evade" the law.

It is inconceivable that a constitutional amendment could be passed in mid-century America authorizing racial segregation, and just as incongruous to think in terms of re-enacting legislation already declared unconstitutional. What the South is really doing lies somewhere between such extremes of "avoidance" and "evasion."

The various legal attempts to avoid the consequences of desegregation fall into . . . [several] categories. Many of the Southern states have reintroduced into the legal scene one or more of the multiple variations of the pre-Civil War doctrines of interposition and nullification. Other states have entered upon a course of legislative action designed to disqualify potential plaintiffs and the NAACP from bringing court actions to end segregation. Still other states have sought to retain separate school systems by changing the theoretical basis of the separation from a classification explicitly based upon race to a classification based upon such factors as "scholastic aptitude," "psychological aptitude" and "free choice." . . .

INTERPOSITION AND NULLIFICATION

Derived from constitutional doctrines first advanced by Jefferson and Madison, the concepts of interposition and nullification have long provided the theoretical basis of the states' rights philosophy. This is the view that the central government is nothing more than a compact between and among the several sovereign states, and that each state has the right to determine the constitutionality of any act of federal authority. In declaring a federal act unconstitutional, a state would be interposing its sovereignty between the central government and the state's own citizens—hence the term interposition.

* * *

Virtually dormant for more than eighty years, these theories have been revived as one aspect of the legal struggle to circumvent the consequences of *Brown v. Board of Education*. It started in Virginia. On January 11, 1956, an interposition act was introduced in the Virginia General Assembly [1] asserting the "right" of the state to maintain a segregated school system. Making obvious reference to *Brown v. Board of Education,* the proposed act declared that the "commonwealth is under no obligation to accept supinely an unlawful decree of the Supreme Court of the United States based upon an authority which is not found in the Constitution of the United States nor any amendment thereto." [2] Three weeks later, the General Assembly restated the compact theory in passing a joint resolution "interposing the sovereignty of Virginia against encroachment upon the reserved powers of this state." [3]

But the resolution meant little more than an expression of dissent —even in Virginia. The state attorney general delivered an opinion as to the "scope, effect, and legal efficacy" of the resolution on February 14, 1956, and admitted its lack of legal validity. While he characterized the legislative action as "far more than a 'stern protest and

---

1. See 1 RACE REL. L. REP. 252 (1956).
2. *Id.*, at 253.
3. Senate Joint Resolution No. 3, General Assembly of Virginia, Feb. 1, 1956. See 1 RACE REL. L. REP. 445 (1956).

a memorial,'" he was forced to give negative answers to the two important legal questions submitted for his opinion:

"6. Is it within the powers of (a) the General Assembly of Virginia by resolution, or (b) the people of Virginia in convention assembled by ordinance, to legally nullify, in whole or in part, the said [Brown v. Board of Education] decision, or to thereby suspend for any period of time its enforcement in Virginia?"

The response of Virginia's attorney general was simply: "a (No), b (No)." [4]

* * *

DISQUALIFYING POTENTIAL LITIGANTS

In the second broad classification of Southern legal action are the various enactments designed to forestall judicial enforcement of the decree of May 31, 1955. The lower federal courts, charged by the Supreme Court with the responsibility for implementation, are powerless to act unless a desegregation suit is in litigation before them. The South is trying to take advantage of this situation by creating legal barriers which would preclude potential plaintiffs' seeking judicial remedies.

Litigation is expensive. Few Southern Negroes could possibly afford to bring suit against school boards in order to obtain admission to all-white elementary and high schools. And, as no governmental agency had taken the initiative in bringing legal proceedings, the task of instituting litigation fell by default to the National Association for the Advancement of Colored People. Where proceedings have been begun in the name of individual Negro school children, it is common knowledge that the NAACP has usually been behind the suit. Consequently, an important part of the Southern legal strategy has been to prevent the NAACP from operating in the deep South.

Three devices have been used to gain this end. The first involved court actions brought by state attorneys general seeking to enjoin the NAACP from any activities within the state. . . .

4. Opinion of the Attorney General, State of Virginia, Feb. 14, 1956. See 1 RACE REL. L. REP. 462, 464 (1956).

A second method of undermining the NAACP is through its members. South Carolina has taken the lead in this area, enacting legislation [5] prohibiting the employment of any NAACP member by a state agency. The statute also provides for a fine against any person hiring a NAACP member for a public post.

Criminal sanctions, obviously directed against the NAACP, represent the third line of attack. . . .

In addition to their campaign against the NAACP, the Southern states have taken legislative action to harass others who would assist potential plaintiffs—as well as the potential plaintiffs themselves. One of the many Virginia plans [6] to circumvent the Supreme Court's determination requires each plaintiff in a state court desegregation proceeding to prepare a long and complicated statement, listing the organizations and individuals who have provided advice or contributed funds in the suit. Failure to reveal the names of those assisting in the litigation—and even failure to comply completely with the vaguely worded statutory requirements—may subject the would-be plaintiffs to judicial punishment. Even where a potential plaintiff is able to comply with the rules, he may be reluctant to do so. . . .

*　　*　　*

SEPARATION—BUT NOT BY RACE

The third general approach to avoiding the consequences of *Brown v. Board of Education* is an attempt to find some method of classification ostensibly devoid of racial overtones—which will still result in the continued separation of the races in the Southern school systems. Many of the Southern states believe that they have found the desired classification factor.

One of the reasons given for the decision of May 17, 1954, was that separate schools "deprive the children of the minority group of equal educational opportunities." Segregated education is more than

5. Act No. 920, General Assembly of South Carolina, 1956. See 1 RACE REL. L. REP. 600 (1956); Act No. 741, General Assembly of South Carolina, 1956. See 1 RACE REL. L. REP. 751 (1956).
6. Act 670 of 1956. 22 VA. CODE § 22-10.1.

a century old, and in the absence of equal educational opportunities, most Negro pupils are considerably less advanced than white children of the same age and school grade. By setting up a classification factor based upon scholastic achievement, the Southern states would be creating a dividing line which would separate white and Negro school children in by far the majority of cases.

This method of classification has been supplemented by the amorphous test of "aptitude." . . .

* * *

Mississippi and Virginia have also enacted legislation setting up classification tests which appear to be nonracial in character.

While the Mississippi statute makes reference to "the educational needs and welfare of the child involved," it puts primary emphasis on "health and moral factors." [7] In order to provide a moral basis which would justify racial segregation, the Mississippi legislature passed another statute which takes advantage of the prevalent disregard for marriage licenses in large parts of the state. Deeply religious, many of the people of rural Mississippi are married by a duly ordained minister of the gospel, but few ever register such marriages with the office of the county clerk. In the eyes of governmental authority, such marriages are deemed common law marriages—both recognized and respected until 1956. Now the State of Mississippi has abolished common law marriages and has declared "any children born as a result thereof illegitimate." [8] This statute applies to the whites as well as to the Negroes of the "Bible Belt," but it is unlikely that it will result in any investigation of the marriage contract of the parents of the white children who apply for admission to the schools.

The test of "aptitude" also appears in the legislation proposed in 1955 by the Gray Commission in Virginia. Giving local school boards all pupil assignment responsibilities, the statute authorizes these boards "to take into consideration such factors as availability of facil-

7. Sec. 6334-02, MISSISSIPPI CODE ANN. (1942).
8. House Bill No. 13, Mississippi Legislature, Regular Session, 1956. See 1 RACE REL. L. REP. 434 (1956).

ities, health, aptitude of the child and the availability of transportation." [9]

All these plans are constitutionally valid—if they are literally enforced without regard to race or color. And whether or not any of these statutes will be held constitutional must depend upon a factual determination. The key is not whether race is omitted as a classification factor, but whether race is truly disregarded in the process of enforcement.

*　　*　　*

Recognizing the constitutional infirmities of these classification schemes, Virginia's Gray Commission recommended a final statutory provision, "that no child be required to attend an integrated school." [10] Virginia seeks to implement this policy by either of two methods.

Under one aspect of the Virginia plan, any child who objects to his assignment to a nonsegregated school has a "free choice" to attend a segregated school. Theoretically, this would result in the maintenance of three separate school systems: white, Negro and mixed. As a practical matter, however, since adherence to the Virginia "way of life" would result in objections by substantially all the white children assigned to integrated schools, the state would continue to run the same sort of segregated school organization as it operated prior to *Brown* v. *Board of Education*. The fact that the Virginia plan really provides for the continuation of the traditional Negro-white school separation is further evidenced by resolutions passed by various county school boards in 1956. These boards have provided that no public revenue will be used for the support of "public schools in said count[ies] wherein white and colored children are taught together under any plan or arrangement whatsoever." [11]

9. Report of Commission on Public Education (Gray Commission), Virginia, Aug. 30, 1954. See 1 RACE REL. L. REP. 241, 242 (1956).
10. *Supra,* note 9, 1 RACE REL. L. REP. 241, 243.
11. Resolution of Board of Supervisors, Prince Edward County, Virginia, May 3, 1956. See 1 RACE REL. L. REP. 780 (1956). Resolution of Board of Supervisors, Loudoun County, Virginia, Aug. 6, 1956. See 1 RACE REL. L. REP. 940 (1956).

As a second means of effectuating the Virginia policy, provision has been made for the payment of tuition grants to those children who object to attending an integrated school and who are unable to find a segregated public school in the local area. This would have the effect of creating a state-wide system of new "private-public" schools such as has been proposed by many of the Southern states as a means of avoiding desegregation.

The decision of May 17, 1954, was directed only against state action which required or permitted racial discrimination. Nothing was said—or could be said—about all-white or all-Negro private schools. Southern lawyers thus hope to avoid desegregation through the device of separating the schools from the states. It is their view that constitutionally they can do indirectly what they cannot do directly: that is, give Southern children segregated education by appropriating state funds to be given to the pupils for tuition rather than appropriating those same funds to maintain the public schools.

*   *   *

If South Carolina *completely* abandons its public school system and makes no provision for any alternate system of education, it will have effectively avoided the consequences of *Brown* v. *Board of Education*. If, on the other hand, South Carolina pursues its present plan of closing a public school whenever a court orders the admission of a Negro to a particular school, the whole scheme will probably be held unconstitutional. At such time as the state would have closed down some schools and would still be operating others, it obviously would be denying some of its school children—both white and colored—the equal protection of the laws.

*   *   *

Under the Virginia plan, on the other hand, the schools which would educate the children who had received state tuition grants would be schools which had always been private in character. And whether or not racial segregation would be constitutionally valid in those private schools would depend upon whether the Supreme

Court held that the receipt of the tuition grants from the states by those institutions transformed them into state agencies for the purposes of the Fourteenth Amendment.

*   *   *

It is probable that the Supreme Court will go even further in extending the application of the present meaning of state action. Language indicating this trend was used by Chief Justice Warren and Justices Black and Douglas in a dissenting opinion during the summer of 1956. "[T]he courts may not be implicated in . . . a discriminatory scheme," wrote the dissenters. "Once the courts put their imprimatur on such a contract, government, speaking through the judicial branch, acts. . . . And it is governmental action that the Constitution controls." [12] This represents an extremely broad reading of the restrictive covenant case of *Shelley* v. *Kraemer* where the Supreme Court declared that the state could not enforce private discriminations. For in the Warren-Black-Douglas view, any slight participation by any state instrumentality in a discriminatory scheme —no matter how limited that "participation"—is unconstitutional state action.

The rule of law that state-imposed racial discrimination is unconstitutional may well result in decisions of future Supreme Courts declaring the invalidity of the racial discrimination now practiced legally by privately operated schools, privately operated businesses and privately operated clubs. This can be done in one of two ways: either by applying the existing law to new factual situations, or by changing the present legal meaning of state action.

*   *   *

It was not until the Supreme Court issued its implementation decree of May 31, 1955, that even the most astute of lawyers became aware of the far-reaching implications of the *School Segregation Cases*. It was only by studying the 1955 determination that the 1954 decision could be understood. And it was not until 1956 that it be-

12. Black v. Cutter Laboratories, 351 U.S. 292, 302, 76 Sup. Ct. 824, 829, 100 L. Ed. 681, 688 Adv. (1956).

came obvious that all state-imposed racial discrimination had been declared unconstitutional *per se*.

But a real understanding of what the nine men said and did on May 17, 1954, goes far beyond the issue of school segregation and far beyond its attendant legal implications. Regardless of personal feelings about racial segregation and regardless of social attitudes toward the Supreme Court's approach and conclusion, *Brown v. Board of Education* must be acknowledged as an important, existing fact. While no attempt has been made within these pages to arrive at sociological judgments as to the rights and wrongs of segregation, there is no discounting the fact that the Supreme Court has spoken and that the law has been determined. Whatever may be done in the future to advance or delay the course of desegregation must be accomplished within the legal framework of this decision. *Brown v. Board of Education* must stand as the most significant civil rights decision ever rendered by an American court and as the symbol of the social revolution which marks mid-twentieth-century America.

ROBERT H. BIRKBY

The Supreme Court and the Bible Belt:
Tennessee Reaction to the "Schempp" Decision

* * *

If the *Schempp* decision had any effect in Tennessee it should be noticeable in the policies adopted and enforced at the school district level. The State Commissioner of Education was reported as saying that it was permissible to read the Bible in public schools despite *Schempp* but he left the final decision to local school officials.[1] The school boards were left free to continue the practice required by state law or to comply with the Court's ruling. This study was undertaken to determine what the school boards did and, if possible, why. Even though it was expected that, in Gordon Patric's words, the "decision was put into effect in diverse ways and 'obeyed' to varying degrees," [2] board action in response to *Schempp* was classified as changing or not changing policy. All districts reporting a departure from the pre-*Schempp* provisions of state law were considered changing districts. It was believed that one of several factors could be used to explain the differences between changing and non-changing districts. These were degree of urbanization, extent of religious pluralism, articulate opposition within the district to devotional exercises, or

1. *Nashville Tennessean*, August 23, 1963, p. 1. In an interview October 16, 1964, the Commissioner confirmed that he had left the decision to local officials. He said at that time that he had taken no official position on the issue.
2. Gordon Patric, "The Impact of a Court Decision: Aftermath of the McCollum Case," 6 *Journal of Public Law*, 455 (1957).

From the *Midwest Journal of Political Science*, 10 (Aug. 1966), pp. 304–15. Reprinted by permission of the Wayne State University Press and the author.

Robert H. Birkby is Associate Professor of Political Science at Vanderbilt University.

differences in the socio-economic composition of the school boards.[3]

To test these suppositions three questionnaires were prepared and sent out in late 1964 and early 1965. One was mailed to each of the 152 superintendents of schools in the state. The second was mailed to the chairman and two other randomly selected members of each school board. The third was sent to the remaining school board members in those districts from which responses were obtained to either or both of the first two questionnaires. The superintendents were asked what the policy on Bible reading and devotional exercises had been in their district before June, 1963, and what it currently was. They were asked to identify any factors inducing change and to describe, in each time period, the policy-making role of the board, superintendent, principals, teachers, parents, religious groups, and any other participants. The first group of board members was asked about current (post 1963) policy, how it differed from that of the past, what groups or persons made policy suggestions to the board, and what groups or persons were consulted by the board. The second group of board members was simply asked to supply information on age, occupation, education, income, religious affiliation, length of service on the board, and length of residence in the school district of its members. Response to the first and third questionnaires was good. . . .

Of the 121 districts, 70 were reported to be still following the requirements of state law. The other 51 districts were reported to have made some changes in their policy but only one of these completely eliminated all Bible reading and devotional exercises. The other 50 merely made student participation voluntary and left the decision whether to have devotional exercises to the discretion of the classroom teacher. Thus 42 percent of the reporting school districts no longer adhere strictly to the provisions of state law even though all but one could have some form of classroom devotional exercise.

The most reasonable explanation for these differences in response to *Schempp* seemed to lie in the extent of urbanization. Table 1 shows the distribution of changing and non-changing districts according to this factor.

3. Daniel F. Boles, *The Bible, Religion and the Public Schools,* 3rd ed. (Ames: Iowa State University Press, 1965). The author suggests (p. 340) the urbanization and religious pluralism explanations.

Table 1

RELATIONSHIP OF URBANIZATION AND SCHOOL RELIGIOUS EXERCISE
POLICY CHANGE

% of District Population Urbanized *	Number of Districts	
	Changing	Not Changing
90–100	17	19
80–89	1	0
70–79	0	0
60–69	0	0
50–59	1	0
40–49	3	1
30–39	2	0
20–29	5	9
10–19	3	4
0–9	19	37
Totals	51	70

* On the basis of 1960 census data.

Using the point bi-serial correlation [4] the relationship between urbanization and tendency toward partial compliance with *Schempp* was found to be practically non-existent ($r_{pb} = -0.08$). Thus, on the basis of questionnaire responses, school boards and superintendents in urban areas showed no greater tendency to change Bible reading and devotional exercise policy than the respondents from rural areas.

The possibility that increasing religious pluralism may account for objections to religion in the schools must remain largely in the realm of speculation since accurate figures on denominational membership by school district or even county do not exist. The National Council of Churches has issued a rough compilation by counties and in lieu of anything else these figures were used to test this possibility. Only those counties with a single area-wide school district (no city districts) and those counties in which the county district and the city district took the same position could be used. This distorts the results somewhat but was made necessary by the impossibility of breaking county religious affiliation figures down into smaller units. On this rough test there is only slight correlation between religious pluralism and tendency to change ($r_{pb} = 0.02$). The pattern of change classified

4. Allen L. Edwards, *Statistical Methods for the Behavioral Sciences* (New York: Rinehart & Company, 1954), pp. 182–85.

by total population of the district was also checked on the theory that heavily populated districts would be more likely to be religiously heterogeneous; again only a slight correlation was found ($r_{pb} = 0.24$).

The other two possibilities advanced above are equally ineffective in explaining the pattern of change. From only one of the eighty-four districts represented by responses from the first group of board members was there a report that the board had been approached by an individual who objected to a continuation of the Bible reading and devotional exercises. In this instance the protester's efforts were in vain since that district still complies with state law. Either there was no significant opposition to devotional exercise or else no board member wanted to admit that there had been any.

Using the chi square test and rejecting the null hypothesis at the 0.01 level of significance, tabulation of the responses of the second group of board members produced no significant differences in socio-economic characteristics between changing and non-changing boards. . . .

In each instance the null hypothesis must be accepted.

Thus far this paper has presented only negative results. Partial compliance with *Schempp* is not explained by degree of urbanization. There are no significant differences in the socio-economic characteristics of changing and non-changing board members. In the changing districts the board members did not report any overt pressure for compliance. And, by a rough test, the extent of religious pluralism in the district had no effect. These findings are significant and justify reporting. It may well be that the population of the State of Tennessee is too homogeneous—socially, religiously, and economically—for any of these tests to be significant. In some other state with greater diversity, urbanization and religious pluralism might be more important. Even so, Tennessee reaction would remain unexplained.

The reported response by Tennessee school districts to *Schempp* might be explained by one other hypothesis. There is in the questionnaires some support for it but not enough to make it possible to assert that it is correct. What follows then is largely speculative. The line of reasoning starts with a distinction between procedural and substantive change in policy. Policy change in any situation may take the form of (1) altering procedure without altering the policy goal, (2) changing procedure to reach a new policy goal without, however, making the new goal explicit, or (3) changing the policy goal with or without a change in procedure. Although we cannot be sure, it seems fairly safe to say that in the fifty school districts which overtly changed their policy on Bible reading and delegated the decision to the teachers there has been little change in fact. That is, it is suspected that the classroom teachers are "voluntarily" conducting Bible reading and devotional exercises just as they did before *Schempp*.[5] One might go a step further and assert, without being able to prove it, that the school boards were aware that this would probably happen. I am suggesting that the board members acted consciously either to save the substance of the program or to avoid upsetting the community status quo by making slight procedural changes. In the language of Sayre and Kaufman, the contestants who had the prizes of the game were able to keep them by responding to a rules change with a rules change of their own.[6] A comment by a lawyer on the board of a changing district indicates the compromise nature of the policy adopted:

> My personal conviction is that the Supreme Court decisions are correct, and I so told the Board and Superintendent; but I saw no reason to create controversy. If the Board had made public a decision abolishing devotional exercises, there would have been public outcry. I believe all staff members understand that the continuance of devotional exercises in their schools and in their rooms is entirely voluntary and subject to discontinuance upon objection of any individual or minority group.

There are other reasons that a board might adopt this strategy of procedural change. It could be used to reduce disagreement within the board itself. It could be suggested by an individual as a means of reducing his own tensions between a desire to comply with the Court's decision and a desire to retain perceived advantages of devotional exercises. Finally, change in procedure without change in

5. This suspicion is based on unsystematic conversations with classroom teachers from two or three districts which made this formal change and on the questionnaire responses of a few superintendents who indicated doubt that any actual change had occurred.
6. Wallace S. Sayre and Herbert Kaufman, *Governing New York City* (New York: Russell Sage Foundation, 1960).

substance might be made to forestall demands for even greater change. There is nothing in the questionnaire responses to indicate which of these alternatives is correct and it is possible that all were present to some extent. If any or all of these suppositions are correct, a desire to retain the program rather than religious pluralism and urbanization would be responsible for the formal change. To this point the hypothesis does not provide an answer to the question of why the form was changed in some districts and not in others. It does emphasize that the answer must be sought in psychological rather than in demographic or socio-economic factors.

The question being asked in any impact study is why the Court's decision is not self-executing. In a different context Richard Neustadt has concluded that a self-executing order must have five characteristics: (1) the issuer of the order must be unambiguously involved in making the decision, (2) the order must be unambiguously worded, (3) the order must receive wide publicity, (4) those receiving the order must have control of the means of implementation, and (5) there must be no doubt of the individual's authority to issue the order.[7] Neustadt was speaking of orders issued by the President but there is no reason that the same analysis cannot be applied to Court decisions. In this instance, there was no doubt that the Court did in fact make the decision though one school board member suggested that the Court was "controlled by small pressure groups." When applied to the Tennessee statute the wording of the order, although negative in content, was clear enough.[8] There was wide publicity. The members of the boards of education had control of the means of implementation. However, the fifth factor was not so obviously present.

There was some confusion about the Court's decision. It was clear enough that required devotional exercises were forbidden but the Court did not commit itself on the status of voluntary programs such

---

7. Richard E. Neustadt, *Presidential Power* (New York: John Wiley and Sons, 1960), p. 19.
8. In some instances this criterion will not be met by a decision. The best examples are the confusion resulting from the "with all deliberate speed" formula in school desegregation and general ambiguity in the majority opinion in *Zorach v. Clauson*, 343 U.S. 306 (1952). See Jack W. Peltason, *Fifty-Eight Lonely Men* (New York: Harcourt, Brace & World, 1961), and Frank J. Sorauf, "*Zorach v. Clauson:* The Impact of a Supreme Court Decision," 53 *American Political Science Review*, 777 (1959).

as those adopted by the fifty changing districts in Tennessee. This ambiguity caused one superintendent to assert confidently "we believe our policy [voluntary participation] is in accordance with the ruling of the Supreme Court and in accord with the desires of the people in this community."

More important is the question of the Court's authority to issue the order. The policy maker's reaction to a judicial decision will be conditioned by his perception of the Court's role in general, his beliefs concerning the importance of the challenged activity or program, his perception of the attitudes of his reference groups and constituents on the issue, and his perception of his role. The differences in policy position may be the result of a general attitude toward the Court and its role in the American system of government.[9] The following comments are typical in content and intensity.

> *Changing Districts*
> *A Surgeon:* We must conform with Federal law. If we are to teach our children to obey laws we must set an example.
> *A Farmer:* We did not want to violate any federal law.
> *A Superintendent:* I think the Supreme Court is correct. Very few people understand the religious issue, less seem to understand what is meant by religious freedom, and relatively few seem to understand the Supreme Court's role in our government.
> *A Farmer:* We are commanded by the Bible to be subject to civil powers as long as their laws do not conflict with laws of God.
>
> *Non-Changing Districts*
> *A Superintendent:* Impeach Earl Warren.
> *A Housewife:* The decision of the Supreme Court seemed senseless and I could see no advantage in making changes.

---

9. Speaking to the American Philosophical Society in 1952, Justice Felix Frankfurter observed that "broadly speaking, the chief reliance of law in a democracy is the habit of popular respect for law. Especially true is it that law as promulgated by the Supreme Court ultimately depends upon confidence of the people in the Supreme Court as an institution." Frankfurter, *Of Law and Men* (New York: Harcourt, Brace & Co., 1956), p. 31. Brehm and Cohen report an experiment demonstrating that the more credible the source of a communication the greater the change in the recipient's attitude even when there was wide discrepancy between the recipient's initial attitude and the content of the communication. Jack W. Brehm and Arthur R. Cohen, *Explorations in Cognitive Dissonance* (New York: John Wiley and Sons, 1962), pp. 247–48.

A College Professor: The Supreme Court decision didn't mean a damn.

A Banker: The general public in this country do not have the respect for the U. S. Supreme Court as they once did. They think it is packed, so to speak, and doubt very much if all are qualified and unbiased and listen to the whims of the President that gave them the appointment. The standards are on a lower level than back several years ago.

A Superintendent: I am at a loss to understand the necessity for this survey. I am of the opinion that 99% of the people in the United States feel as I do about the Supreme Court's decision— that it was an outrage and that Congress should have it amended. The remaining 1% do not belong in this free world.

A Lawyer: We felt that in the absence of some good specific objection, there was no compelling reason to change previous policy.

If one had these comments without information on the policy adopted, it would not be too difficult to predict the position taken by each of these school boards.

The Court-attitude is only one of the variables affecting the impact of a judicial decision. The other major variable is the policy maker's assessment of and commitment to the challenged program or activity. . . .

*   *   *

Perceptions of the attitudes of constituents or clientele are important but seem to be secondary. They play the role of reinforcing or modifying the Court-attitude and/or the program-attitude. A dentist on the board of a changing district observed that "we thought public opinion would want us to comply with Federal Law," while a chairman of a non-changing board (who did not indicate his occupation) said that the most important factor influencing him was that "we would have had complaints if we did not have Bible reading." Both of these board members were reacting to their perception of constituent attitude. . . .

*   *   *

On the basis of the information available, it is impossible to weigh the value of the perceptions that went into the making of the policies.

But one might hazard a guess that in the changing districts a perception of the Court as an authoritative body exercising legitimate power was strong enough to override any commitment to devotional exercises. The reverse, of course, would hold true in non-changing districts. The weight given to reference group attitudes and the direction of those attitudes probably, though not necessarily, varied in the same direction as the final policy decision and served to reinforce attitudes toward the Court or beliefs in the value of devotionals. That is, public opinion in changing districts probably was perceived by the board as favoring or at least not opposing compliance with *Schempp* and strengthened the board's desire to comply.

One warning is in order. It is not asserted that procedural change to save substance and intensity of attitude explains what took place in Tennessee. All that is claimed here is that with the failure of the initial hypotheses in this study this additional explanation is possible and is supported to some extent by the response to the questionnaires.

*   *   *

RICHARD M. JOHNSON

Compliance and Supreme Court Decision-Making

The United States Supreme Court has been concerned with many explosive social issues since World War II, but the decisions affecting perhaps more Americans more intimately than any others are those dealing with the place of religion in society. The Court, on a number of well-publicized occasions, has been forced to examine religious involvement in public education and decide what the first amendment's vague "establishment" clause would allow.[1] The course that the Court has followed on these occasions has brought serious misgivings to individuals of deep religious conviction. Prominent church leaders—from former Episcopal Bishop James Pike, to Cardinal Cushing, to evangelist Billy Graham—have spoken out against the Court's policy; congressmen, senators, and state officials have attempted official action to offset it; and communities have expressed their antagonism in a variety of ways.[2] Americans from all walks of life have been forced to think more abstractly about the nexus between their government and that which is very close to them: their relationship to the Almighty.

. . . This article studies Supreme Court *decision-making*. How-

1. School Dist. v. Schempp, 374 U.S. 203 (1963) Engel v. Vitale, 370 U.S. 421 (1962); Zorach v. Clauson, 343 U.S. 306 (1952); Illinois *ex rel.* McCollum v. Board of Educ., 333 U.S. 203 (1948); Everson v. Board of Educ., 330 U.S. 1 (1947).

2. See, *e.g.*, Editorial, *Politics of Prayer Stir the Nation,* 79 CHRISTIAN CENTURY 856 (1962); *Uproar Over School Prayer—And the Aftermath,* U.S. News and World Report, July 9, 1962, p. 42.

From the *Wisconsin Law Review,* Volume 1961, No. 1 (Winter 1967), pp. 170–85. Reprinted by permission of the publisher and the author.

Richard M. Johnson is Assistant Professor of Political Science at the State University of New York (SUNY) at Buffalo.

ever, little attention will be paid to the Court, for we shall concern ourselves primarily with how individuals in a community have responded to what the Court has said. Decision-making, therefore, is being quite broadly defined to encompass a variety of actors. A decision is viewed as

> an *effective* determination of policy . . . [involving] the total process of bringing about a specified course of action. . . . [T]he decision-making process includes application as well as formulation and promulgation of policy, [consequently] those whose acts are affected also participate in decision-making: by conformity to or disregard of the policy they help determine whether it is or is not in fact a decision. Laws are not made by legislatures alone, but by the law-abiding as well: a statute ceases to embody a law . . . in the degree that it is widely disregarded.[3]

Thus, for a judicial policy to have general effect in the political system, the behavior of many individuals must be affected.

Religious observances or exercises in one form or another have been quite common in the public schools of America.[4] Whether such practices are prohibited according to the Court's general test—that is, if they have a primary effect that advances religion [5]—will be decided by individuals at the local level, most often by school administrators. In making this decision, school administrators become agents in the judicial process. Only in an extremely limited number of cases, and probably only in religiously heterogeneous communities, will legal mechanisms be energized to make school district practices conform with the Court's policy. In religiously homogeneous communities, religious practices probably have continued in public school classrooms, unabated by the Court's policies. Even inaction on the part of the administrator or deliberate action to disregard Court policy has consequences for the judicial process in its broader aspects.[6]

On the other hand, even though the community is more or less united in the belief that there should be some religious worship or observance in classrooms, school officials may still recognize a para-

3. LASSWELL & KAPLAN, POWER AND SOCIETY 74–75 (1950).
4. See, *e.g.*, DIERENFIELD, RELIGION IN AMERICAN PUBLIC SCHOOLS (1962).
5. School Dist. v. Schempp, 374 U.S. 203, 222 (1963).
6. The importance of "non-decision" is stressed in Bachrach & Baratz, *Decisions and Nondecisions: An Analytical Framework*, 57 AM. POL. SCI. REV. 632 (1963).

mount responsibility to bring practices in their schools into perceived congruence with the policy enunciated by the Court. What happens when a school official makes such a decision?

A new superintendent of a rural school district in central Illinois (which we shall call Eastville) halted the saying of a prayer before lunch in the school cafeteria. He felt that the prayer was repugnant personally and clearly contrary to his understanding of the *Engel* [7] and *Schempp* [8] decisions. Yet community conflict did not follow in this very homogeneous, fundamentalist Protestant community. The following data—derived from a structured questionnaire mailed to all Eastville school district parents, school officials, teachers, and community "influentials"—suggests an explanation that is based solely upon the psychological dimension: the substance and distribution of attitudes toward the Court, its policies, and local practices found in Eastville.[9]

Acquiescence by the Eastville community was somewhat surprising, even to some of its residents and school officials. The community is a religious one, and this religiosity affected the public school system. The lunchtime prayer was just one of its manifestations.[10] In the interviews, respondent after respondent indicated that the prayers were held because they were expressive of the desires of the community.

Acquiescence, then, did not result from individuals *personally* accepting and agreeing with the Supreme Court decisions. Roughly one-quarter reported that they agreed personally with the Court's policy regarding religious practices in public schools. Indeed, over seventy percent of the respondents felt that the Supreme Court had exceeded its range of power in this matter, while less than twenty

7. Engel v. Vitale, 370 U.S. 421 (1962).
8. School Dist. v. Schempp, 374 U.S. 203 (1963).
9. For a full report of this study, see Richard M. Johnson, Separation of Church and State: The Dynamics of Supreme Court Decision-Making, 1965. (unpublished doctoral dissertation in University of Illinois Library).

Three hundred questionnaires were mailed, and 176 were returned, a response rate of nearly 59%. . . .

10. Another manifestation: The Women's Christian Temperance Union gave lectures, showed movies, distributed literature, and sponsored an annual poster contest in which the students extolled the virtues of temperance and emphasized that liquor and cigarettes were the antithesis of Jesus Christ. Winning posters were prominently displayed in the windows of Eastville merchants.

percent acknowledged that the issue was one properly to be handled by the Court. For a majority, the Court's *Engel* and *Schempp* rulings were viewed as assisting feared "godless groups" and fitted a "general trend in this country toward godlessness, corruption, crime, divorce, and delinquency."

Despite this lack of *personal acceptance* of the decisions and the perceived negative implications, fifty-five percent of the respondents having an opinion did acknowledge the necessity for public compliance with them. Thus, there are a large number of people who personally disagree with what the Court has said but who feel that they must comply regardless of their personal views on the issue. Private acceptance and the recognition of an obligation of public compliance are not two sides of the same coin.

Since this recognition of a duty of public compliance does not automatically follow from personal acceptance of the substance of the policy, let us consider the various ways in which individuals may respond to the Court's decisions. Treating both of these dimensions in terms of a three point (agree–neutral–disagree) scale, there are theoretically nine different modes of response, ranging from "private acceptance" and "public compliance" to "personal rejection" coupled with "denial of a duty of public compliance." While there are these nine possible attitudinal combinations, Table 1 shows that only seven

Table 1

BASIC MODES OF RESPONSE TO COURT INTERPRETATION AND
RESPECTIVE FREQUENCIES

Public Compliance *	Private Acceptance **		
	Agree	Neutral	Disagree
Agree	A (39)	C (16)	E (30)
Neutral		G (5)	
Disagree	B (4)	D (11)	F (54)

* *Public Compliance:* "No matter what one may think about religious practices, if the Supreme Court says they are unconstitutional, one has the duty to accept the decision and act accordingly."

** *Private Acceptance:* "Do you agree or disagree with what the Court has said about religious practices in public schools?"

were found empirically.[11] Those found empirically are given letter designations from A to G as illustrated in Table 1.

Table 1 shows that 85 out of 159 respondents—nearly fifty-seven percent—recognized the duty to comply with Court policy. The distribution of these attitudes is more important than the gross figures, however. Table 2 indicates that important people in the system are found in those categories involving the notion of public compliance. A number of important actors are mode A respondents. More teachers are found in mode A than in any other category, and the same is true for the community "influentials." [12] Most of the remaining occupants of special systemic roles are found in those modes of response that entail a recognition of a duty to comply.

Table 2

COMPOSITION OF MODE OF RESPONSE CATEGORIES

Roles	Modes of Response						
	A	B	C	D	E	F	G
Community Totals	39	4	16	11	30	54	5
Superintendent	1						
Former Superintendent					1		
School Board	2		2		1	2	
Principals	3					1	
Teachers	11				6	7	
"Influentials"	13	2	2	1	6	10	

This analysis helps us to understand how the new superintendent could come into a highly traditional religious community and upset a desired custom without incurring the wrath of the community.[13]

11. For the following analysis, only those respondents who indicated an opinion on both the private acceptance and public compliance dimensions are considered.

12. The index of personal influence used is the following item: "Compared with other people you know, are you more or less likely to be asked for information or advice about these matters [court decisions involving religious practices in the schools]?" Slightly over 20% of the respondents designated themselves as being influential in this regard. This use of self-designation of opinion leadership is patterned after the approach utilized in KATZ & LAZARSFELD, PERSONAL INFLUENCE 261 (1955).

13. It should be noted that the former superintendent, in the wake of Engel v. Vitale, 370 U.S. 421 (1962), had declared that he would change practices in his school district only "if they placed a policeman at the door to the school." Interview With Former Superintendent.

Extensive support for such action apparently already existed, especially among important actors in the community. This body of support lay dormant until tapped by the superintendent; in reality, forces that already existed were mobilized to support compliance with the Court's policy. If antagonisms existed in the community, they did not become vocal, possibly because no leadership was provided among community or school leaders.

THE DYNAMICS OF RESPONSE

Table 1 indicates a great range of response in the Eastville community, from those who personally accepted the decisions and expected public compliance to those who rejected the decisions and objected to public compliance with them. There are distinct attitudinal clusters associated with each mode of response that partially account for such variation.

Seventeen items included in the questionnaire were designed to tap various bases of acceptance or rejection of Supreme Court policy.[14] Upon analysis, there emerged a theoretically significant pattern of response that may be used to explain more clearly the mode of response categories discussed above. Through the mathematical technique of factor analysis, four theoretically significant factors were extracted from these responses.[15] The nature of these factors is deter-

14. For a discussion of the theory underlying the individual items see Richard M. Johnson, *op. cit. supra* note 9, at ch. 1 ("Introduction: Decision-making and the Supreme Court").

15. Factor analysis is based upon the idea that when there are a number of interrelated variables or indices, "these interrelationships may be due to the presence of one or more underlying variables or *factors* which are related to the indices to varying degrees." BLALOCK, SOCIAL STATISTICS 383 (1960). For a brief but clear explanation of this technique, see *id.* at 383-91. A much more detailed account may be found in FRUCHTER, INTRODUCTION TO FACTOR ANALYSIS (1954).

In factor analysis, one begins with a matrix of correlations wherein each item is correlated with every other item. Here, the responses to the seventeen questionnaire items were correlated. Factors are then extracted in the order in which they explain statistically the variation of the items. The original factors are "rotated" to obtain factors that have some psychological meaning. The rotation provides factors that are highly correlated with certain items while being uncorrelated with others. For this analysis, the Centroid Factor Analysis program and the Varimax Factor Rotation program for an IBM 7090 computer

mined by analyzing what the indices correlated with the factor have in common.

The four factors extracted have been termed "local responsibility," "rewards to negative reference groups," "national legitimacy," and "expertise." The first factor is related to a notion of local responsibility insofar as religious practices in public schools are concerned. . . .

*   *   *

The second factor pertains to the notion that the Supreme Court's *Engel* and *Schempp* rulings constitute "rewards to negative reference groups." Not only do the rulings reward individuals and groups that are patently alien to one's own religious values, but they are actually part and parcel of the dreaded trend in this nation toward secularism and its attendant evils. . . .

*   *   *

The third factor has been termed "national legitimacy." Each of the questionnaire items most strongly correlated with it involve some aspect of preferring national norms to local norms and practices. . . .

*   *   *

The final factor is involved with the notion of the Court's collective expertise. One item clearly refers to the expertise of the justices that accrues from their specialized training. . . .

*   *   *

One item apparently has little connection with the other two items that correlate highly with this factor. It was originally included to tap the notion of coercive power. But the inclusion of this item in the expertise factor is theoretically tenable. The workings of the court system in general is beyond the experience and comprehension of most people. When a conflict reaches the judiciary for resolution, it

were used. Both the programs and the technical help were supplied by the Statistical Services Unit of the University of Illinois.

enters an arena where the usual rules of the political game do not hold. Judicial activity takes place in a highly contrived setting, esoteric materials and language are used, and the actual decision-making takes place at a point far removed from the public's gaze. All of these facets tend to maintain the distance between the judiciary and the public. Thus, even though individuals may be deeply attached to religious exercises in their public schools, it could very well be that these practices would not stand the test in court. It is ultimately the Court, then, that has the special competence to say whether the practices conform to the Constitution. In this sense, one may feel powerless to dispute its word. Thus, this item may be considered congruent with others more directly expressive of the notion of expertise.

These factors are rather insignificant in themselves, and they only assume importance insofar as they are useful in understanding the dynamics of the response in Eastville to the Court's decision. Do they help us understand why community conflict did not follow the decision to halt the lunchtime prayers? Each respondent was given a score on each factor by summing his responses to those items that were most highly correlated with each factor. For convenience in comparison, the three items having the highest correlation with the factor were used to determine the individual factor scores. The total score a respondent has received for the three items in each factor constitutes the factor score. Respondents could indicate agreement or disagreement with the statement in terms of a seven point scale, one point indicating strong agreement and seven points indicating strong disagreement, so the factor scores may range from three to twenty-one. The lower scores indicate agreement, the higher scores indicate disagreement, and a score of twelve indicates a neutral position. The respondents scores on the respective factors may be summed, and four mean factor scores derived for each of the modes of response previously identified.[16] If there is any validity at all to the factors that have been extracted, significant differences should exist between the mean factor scores of the various modes of response. For instance, there should be significantly higher mean scores for the local responsibility and negative reference groups factors in mode A, which entails both private acceptance and the duty of public compliance,

16. See Table 1 *supra*.

than in mode F, which entails neither. The reverse situation would be expected when comparing these modes as to their mean scores for the national legitimacy and expertise factors. Probably the most crucial differences are those in the mean factor scores of modes E and F respondents. Both of these types disagree with the rulings, but they differ on acknowledging the necessity for public compliance.

Table 3

MODES OF RESPONSE TO COURT POLICY WITH RESPECTIVE MEAN FACTOR SCORES

Modes of Response *	1. Local Responsibility	2. Rewards to Negative Reference Groups	3. National Legitimacy	4. Expertise
A. Private Acceptance and Public Compliance (N = 39)	16.3 **	15.4	7.8	9.8
B. Private Acceptance, No Public Compliance (N = 4)	14.5	14.3	14.5	15.8
C. Public Compliance, Acceptance Unknown (N = 16)	11.8	10.5	8.4	7.1
D. No Public Compliance, Acceptance Unknown (N = 11)	9.5	9.9	14.0	13.3
E. Public Compliance, No Private Acceptance (N = 30)	12.1	8.7	10.3	11.0
F. Neither Public Compliance nor Private Acceptance (N = 54)	8.4	7.6	14.0	12.3

* Since Mode G, which contains respondents who are completely indifferent on both the private acceptance and public compliance dimensions, is of minor significance both theoretically and numerically, it is not included in this analysis.

** Scores may range from 3 to 21 with low scores indicating agreement. The mid-point or neutral position is 12.

Table 3 presents the modes of response and their respective mean factor scores. We shall focus our analysis primarily upon modes A, E, and F because there is clear-cut agreement or disagreement on private acceptance and public compliance. Mode A has by far the largest mean factor scores on the reward to negative groups and local responsibility factors and the lowest scores on the national legitimacy and expertise factors.

This is understandable. Since the respondents in this category privately agree with what the Court has said about religious practices in public schools, one would expect them to disagree that this is a matter to be handled locally or that the rulings penalize godliness. By the same token, it is not surprising to find these respondents also acknowledging to a greater extent the legitimacy and the expert bases of Court power.

Viewing the mean factor scores in mode E—those who disagree privately but acknowledge a public responsibility for compliance— we see that the strongest mean score is associated with the rewards to negative reference groups factor. Respondents agree that the rulings by the Court are rewarding negative reference groups. On the local responsibility factor, the mean score indicates an indifference as the score stands on dead center. On both the legitimacy and the expertise factors, the mode E mean scores indicate a tendency in the direction of agreement.

As opposed to this, the mean factor scores in mode F—neither private acceptance nor public compliance—indicate strong agreement among respondents on the rewards to negative reference groups and local responsibility factors, with disagreement and neutrality on the legitimacy and expertise factors respectively. The mode F respondents tend to believe that the problem of religious activities in the public schools is properly one of local, not national, concern and that the Court rulings in this matter have rewarded godless groups. These respondents tend to disagree with the legitimacy of the Court in this area and are largely indifferent to the notion that the Court possesses the expertise to make the proper judgments in this, as well as other, areas.

*   *   *

A comparison of factor means between respondents of modes E and F reveals that the two groups do not differ significantly on the reward to negative reference groups and expertise factors. Both groups tend to feel rather strongly that the rulings of the Court reward the forces of godlessness in this country, thus differing significantly from the respondents in mode A.

This may reflect a deeper religious commitment on the part of mode E and F respondents than those in mode A. A comparison of the groups on a "religiosity" factor confirmed that this was true. Mode E and F had significantly lower mean factor scores than mode A.[17]

*　　*　　*

EASTVILLE AND THE LARGER WORLD

The Supreme Court's policy concerning religious practices in public schools ran counter to the prevailing values in the Eastville school district. Nevertheless, the central decision-maker for the school system, who found the policy congruent with his privately held notions, brought the system into a perceived state of compliance with the rulings. Rather than arousing a great deal of controversy, the action was generally supported or accepted in good grace. There are compelling factors that may offset private disagreement with the substance of the Court's policy. The legitimacy of the Court and its expertise are such offsetting factors. While an individual may feel that the ruling is an aid to groups he deplores, he may grudgingly acknowledge the duty to do what the Court has said because it is the appropriate body for making such a determination or because it possesses the necessary skills to discover what the Constitution "really means" in the "establishment" clause of the first amendment. On the other hand, those who stubbornly dispute a duty to comply with the Court's ruling may do so by countering the notion of a national legitimacy surrounding the Court with a notion of local legitimacy—the local system should dictate the solutions to such problems, not some far-off court. In Eastville, however, those acknowledging a duty to

17. This religiosity factor was extracted through a factor analysis of a group of varied attitudinal questions included in the questionnaire. Three of the items were obtained originally from a scale of "religious conventionalism" found in Francesco, *A Pervasive Value: Conventional Religiosity*, 57 J. SOCIAL PSYCHOLOGY 467 (1962). A fourth item was obtained from the "authoritarianism" subscale of Milton Rokeach's "dogmatism" scale in ROKEACH, OPEN AND CLOSED MIND 77 (1960). . . .

comply with the rulings are in the majority, particularly so in the case of the community "influentials." [18] Consequently, the superintendent actually had a rather firm basis of support for the action he took; people who may have been antagonistic to this action were left without community leadership around which they could rally.

While the Eastville school district did comply with the Supreme Court's prayer rulings, the substance of this compliant behavior was in a form generally acceptable to this religious community. Certainly the schools of the district did not have shorn from them all vestiges of the deeply religious orientation of the community.[19] Even though an accommodation toward religious observances was made, perhaps the core of the general rule laid down by the Court remained intact: Children were not to be forcibly exposed to the religious views of others through an officially sanctioned prayer in the lunchrooms of the elementary schools.

What happens in the lunchrooms of the Eastville schools vis-à-vis a Supreme Court determination does not mean that in the larger sense there has been an effective decision with respect to the *Schempp* ruling. Before this can be concluded, similar action must be taken throughout the land. It is striking, however, that even in this relatively remote locale—one set apart from modern urban America in many ways (there is not a single lawyer in the community!)—the impact of Supreme Court decision-making has been felt. The policy enunciated by the Court has been transmitted to relevant actors in the local system through channels not ordinarily considered indigenous to the legal order—newspapers, magazines, radio, and television—and action was taken in the absence of a strict and immediate legal obligation. This is perhaps not unique and is probably a quite normal condition. However, social science research tends to focus upon the unique: the conflict situations, the times when local communities do not comply, and the litigation to force compliance with Court policy. Thus these "normal" processes are neglected by researchers.

A final point concerning the notion of "compliance" should be made. Supreme Court policy in the area of religious exercise in

18. See Table 2 *supra.*
19. See note 9 *supra.*

public schools invoked a range of responses in Eastville, each of the several modes of response observed having an underlying attitudinal structure that justified it. The superintendent could justify changing overt behavior on the ground that such change was required by Supreme Court policy. However, his predecessor could similarly justify discrepant behavior because of a local responsibility for providing for the religious health of the community's children. Thus, the term "compliance" seems to suggest a single approved response to a Court ruling. . . .

*   *   *

One runs afoul, however, when one views Court rulings in their broadest contexts. A much more complex set of problems arise when dealing with instances that have not been *directly* the subject of litigation. The Court has stated that a school board may not prescribe that a prayer be said [20] or that the Bible be read in devotional services in public schools.[21] Does compliance with this mean that a teacher may not lead her students in prayer before lunch in the school's cafeteria? Does this mean that the Bible may not be read and used as history or as a certain literary form in public schools? Can baccalaureate services be held in school auditoriums? Can school children be allowed to use religious motifs in their art work during certain religious seasons of the year?

These are very real problems that must be dealt with by school administrators throughout the nation. As they become aware of the Court policy in these matters through innumerable sources, they may have to evaluate their own programs in light of this national policy. If they perceive a discrepancy existing, they may seek to bring about an accommodation between local practice and national policy. The range of possibilities for such an accommodation is immense and depends in large measure on the social milieu and personal characteristics of relevant decision-makers at the point of implementation. Thus, Samuel Krislov is on point when he notes that "what is or is

20. Engel v. Vitale, 370 U.S. 421 (1962).
21. School Dist. v. Schempp, 374 U.S. 203 (1963).

not compliance belongs in the realm not of 'objective reality' but rather is defined by what is acceptable . . . . [T]he zone of compliance will vary based upon social perception." [22] Such a broad gauge notion of compliance will focus attention on the roles of a wide range of actors in the judicial process.

22. Krislov, *The Perimeters of Power: Patterns of Compliance and Opposition to Supreme Court Decisions,* 1963 (paper delivered to the 1963 Annual Meeting of the American Political Science Association), p. 11.

JAMES P. LEVINE

Constitutional Law and Obscene Literature:
An Investigation of Bookseller Censorship Practices *

Because individual freedoms are central to democratic theory and ideology, it is surprising to discover the paucity of systematic research concerned with conditions supportive of civil liberties. There have been few studies treating the behavioral fact of freedom as a dependent variable, the existence or absence of which is to be explained by politico-legal, sociological, or psychological factors.[1] This study is an exploration of some determinants of one kind of freedom—the freedom to acquire literature dealing with sexual behavior.

Sexual speech was selected as a testing ground for hypotheses

* The author is indebted to the Russell Sage Program in Law and the Social Sciences at Northwestern University for its generous support during all phases of this study. Victor G. Rosenblum deserves special thanks for his useful suggestions and his never-ending encouragement.

1. Exceptions are: Marjorie Fiske, *Book Selection and Censorship* (Berkeley: University of California Press, 1959); Marie Jahoda and Stuart Cook, "Security Measures and Freedom of Thought: An Exploratory Study of the Impact of Loyalty and Security Programs," *Yale Law Journal*, 61 (March 1952), 295–333. Many survey studies of public attitudes toward freedom have accumulated, among which are: Samuel Stouffer, *Communism, Conformity, and Civil Liberties* (New York: Doubleday, 1955); James Prothro and Charles Gregg, "Fundamental Principles of Democracy: Bases of Agreement and Disagreement," *Journal of Politics*, 22 (May 1960), 276–294. Major works dealing with the social determinants of extremist voting behavior are: William Kornhauser, *The Politics of Mass Society* (New York: The Free Press, 1959); Seymour Lipset, *Political Man* (New York: Doubleday, 1963).

This article is based on Mr. Levine's unpublished Ph.D. dissertation, "The Bookseller and the Law of Obscenity: Toward an Empirical Theory of Free Expression" (Northwestern University, 1967) and was written expressly for this volume.

James P. Levine is an Assistant Professor of Political Science at the University of Oregon.

about civil liberties because of the relevance of sex to so many facets of life. The subject of sex is not only an integral part of aesthetic expression (especially in so much of contemporary fiction and drama), but allusions to sex abound in the fields of advertising, entertainment, psychoanalysis, and even religion. We are a highly sex-conscious society.

Bookseller self-censorship practices were used as an index of freedom of sexual speech prevailing in a community. This measure was chosen because books are an important medium of public communications and the retail bookseller plays a vital role in their dissemination. Furthermore, casual observation suggested that variance in the amount of censorship exercised by bookstores was considerable—ranging from ultra-restrictive "Bible shops" that weed out all books making reference to sex to the ultra-permissive "smut shops" which specialize in "pulp" literature focusing on sexual deviance. This variation allows the researcher to observe, measure, and chart, if only imprecisely, the scope of freedom in a society.

A THEORY OF FREE SPEECH

Although our knowledge about the efficacy of law as an instrument of social control is slight, it is frequently urged that constitutional checks on political power, enforced vigorously by judicial institutions, provide the best defense of individual liberties. As early as 1835, Alexis de Tocqueville contended that the American judiciary, with its power of judicial review, was "one of the most powerful barriers which has ever been devised" to prevent mass tyranny.[2] Similarly, implicit in much legal writing of today is the thesis that courts are the major protectors of freedom. Charles Black states this position forthrightly:

> The judicial power is one of the accredited means by which our nation seeks its goals, including the prime goal . . . of self-limitation. Intellectual freedom, freedom from irrational discrimination,

2. Alexis de Tocqueville, *Democracy in America*, trans. Phillips Bradley (New York: Vintage Books, 1954), I, 102–109.

immunity from unfair administration of the law—these (and others similar) are the constitutional interests which the Court can protect on ample doctrinal grounds. They often cannot win protection in rough-and-tumble politics. The Supreme Court is more and more finding its highest institutional role is the guarding of such interests.[3]

Given the multivariate nature of most social scientific explanations, it is likely that notions of judicial omnipotence suffer from oversimplification.[4] Consequently, the perspective taken here is that judicial policy-making is only one of a host of independent variables which relate to the phenomenon of social freedom.

The theory may be stated briefly in propositional form. If appellate courts are permissive in establishing the boundaries of constitutionally protected speech, political elites will be prevented from invoking legal sanctions to suppress speech. If a community is urban and its population is wealthy, educated, mobile, and young, it is likely to have a tolerant climate of public opinion which nullifies customary restraints on speech.

Alternatively, booksellers' personal attitudes toward sexual speech may insulate them from the effects of both law and custom. If the bookseller is tolerant of deviant expression, he will adopt permissive practices, marketing all kinds of books freely; contrariwise, intolerance will lead to restrictive sales policies. This is really a "safety-valve" hypothesis: if the data fail to confirm primary hypotheses about the effects of appellate court behavior and community structure, a high correlation between attitudes of booksellers and censorial practices may help to account for these negative findings.

3. Charles Black, *Perspectives on Constitutional Law* (Englewood Cliffs, New Jersey: Prentice-Hall, 1963), p. 5.
4. Equally implausible are contentions that courts are completely impotent, such as the following assertion made by Judge Learned Hand:

> . . . this much I think I do know—that a society so riven that the spirit of moderation is gone, no court *can* save; that a society where that spirit flourishes no court *need* save; that in a society which evades its responsibility by thrusting upon the courts the nurture of that spirit, that spirit in the end will perish.

The Spirit of Liberty (New York: Vintage Books, 1959), p. 125.

THE ROLE OF THE COURTS

Modern obscenity law was born in 1957 when the United States Supreme Court upheld the constitutionality of federal and state obscenity laws in *Roth v. United States*.[5] The Court side-stepped the delicate problems of the "clear-and-present-danger" test by devising a "two-level free-speech theory." [6] The first step asks whether a communication has any social utility; if the answer is negative, the second step, an evaluation of the clarity, proximity, and gravity of the danger, need not be taken. In the Court's own words:

> All ideas having even the slightest redeeming social importance —unorthodox ideas, controversial ideas, even ideas hateful to the prevailing climate of opinion—have the full protection of the guarantees, unless excludable because they encroach upon the limited areas of more important interests. But implicit in the history of the First Amendment is the rejection of obscenity as utterly without redeeming social importance.[7]

By engaging in some intricate historiography, the Court establishes to its satisfaction that obscenity is, and always has been, outside the coverage of the First Amendment.

Although the constitutionality of restrictions on speech about sex thus hinged on the definition and applicability of the concept of obscenity, the Court was elusive in describing the kind of material falling within this category. Criteria used in thirteen lower court cases were approved, as was the norm advocated by the American Law Institute in its *Model Penal Code*. The proper test of obscenity was said to be:

> whether to the average person, applying contemporary community standards, the dominant theme of the material taken as a whole appeals to prurient interest.[8]

Expertise in constitutional law is not required to recognize the ineffable quality of the terms of this "standard." The Court failed to

5. 354 U.S. 476 (1957).
6. Harry Kalven, "The Metaphysics of the Law of Obscenity," *The Supreme Court Review*, 1960, p. 8.
7. 354 U.S. 476, 484 (1957).
8. 354 U.S. 476, 489 (1957).

provide a neat "pigeon-hole" into which obscene speech could be sorted with any degree of objectivity. In short, the *Roth* opinion avoided grappling with the concrete limits of permissible sexual speech.[9]

However, in a series of subsequent cases, the Court relied on *Roth* to reveal its anti-puritanical posture. From 1957 to 1965, several lower court findings of obscenity were reversed in *per curiam* decisions without opinions. The following specimens of sexual speech were legitimated: (1) imported "art" magazines containing photographs of nude females;[10] (2) *The Game of Love,* a foreign "art" film;[11] (3) homosexual magazines with pictures of scantily-clad males;[12] (4) nudist magazines;[13] (5) *Pleasure Is My Business,* a pocket-book detailing the adventures of a nymphomaniac;[14] (6) Henry Miller's *Tropic of Cancer;*[15] and (7) *A Stranger Knocks,* a Danish film containing implied scenes of sexual intercourse.[16] The terribly abstract verbiage of *Roth* proved to be sufficiently flexible to limit severely the sphere of expression which could be constitutionally banned by the state.

The Supreme Court's post-*Roth* decisions also were permissive. The prohibition of "ideological" or "thematic" obscenity was held unconstitutional in *Kingsley International Pictures v. Regents*[17] in which the Court overturned a censorship board's denial of a license to exhibit the film *Lady Chatterley's Lover* because it depicts adultery in an approving manner. In *Manual Enterprises v. Day*[18] the additional criterion of "patent offensiveness" was tacked on to the requirements of *Roth;* it was held that a magazine including photographs of nude males does not go "beyond the pale of contemporary

9. The Court did, however, create two constitutional requisites which loosened legal restraints on sexual speech: (1) findings of obscenity must be based on the effects of the disputed work on the average adult rather than the most susceptible elements of society; (2) material must be judged as a whole and isolated words and passages cannot be singled out for independent evaluation.
10. *Mounce v. United States,* 355 U.S. 180 (1957).
11. *Times Film Corp. v. Chicago,* 355 U.S. 35 (1957).
12. *One, Inc. v. Oleson,* 355 U.S. 371 (1958).
13. *Sunshine Book Co. v. Summerfield,* 355 U.S. 372 (1958).
14. *Tralins v. Gerstein,* 378 U.S. 576 (1964).
15. *Grove Press v. Gerstein,* 378 U.S. 577 (1964).
16. *Trans-Lux Distributing Corp. v. Regents,* 380 U.S. 259 (1965).
17. 360 U.S. 384 (1959).
18. 370 U.S. 348 (1962).

notions of rudimentary decency" and therefore cannot be excluded from the mails. In 1964, the Court reversed a conviction for exhibiting *Les Amants,* a French film in which an explicit love scene is portrayed, holding that national standards must be used in applying state obscenity statutes.[19] Finally, in 1966, John Cleland's *Memoirs of a Woman of Pleasure,* an example *par excellence* of "erotic realism," [20] was declared non-obscene on the grounds that material must be "utterly without redeeming social importance" to be constitutionally proscribable.[21]

The development of the procedural law of obscenity paralleled the liberal tendency of the Supreme Court's substantive decisions. The use of injunctive remedies to prevent further distribution of materials adjudicated obscene has been sustained,[22] but the Court has used the due process clause to restrict searches and seizures of *allegedly* obscene publications.[23] Similarly, the abstract principle of administrative censorship of motion pictures prior to exhibition has been upheld,[24] but the Court has severely curtailed the discretion of the administrator,[25] thereby pulling the teeth out of many censorship operations.

In 1966, in the case of *Ginzburg v. United States,*[26] the Court reversed directions when it affirmed a conviction for sending erotica through the mails on the ground that the defendant was exploiting the sexual content of the publications and pandering to the sexual instincts of his audience. In a companion case, the Court was also restrictive, holding that the prurient appeal of literature dealing with abnormal sexuality was to be assessed in terms of the sexual interests of its intended and probable primary recipient group, rather than the sexual interests of the average member of the community.[27]

19. *Jacobellis v. Ohio,* 378 U.S. 184 (1964).
20. Eberhard Kronhausen and Phyllis Kronhausen, *Pornography and the Law* (New York: Ballantine Books, 1964), pp. 303–324.
21. *Memoirs v. Massachusetts,* 383 U.S. 413 (1966).
22. *Kingsley Books v. Brown,* 354 U.S. 436 (1957).
23. *Marcus v. Search Warrants of Property,* 367 U.S. 717 (1961); *A Quantity of Books v. Kansas,* 378 U.S. 205 (1964).
24. *Times Film Corp. v. Chicago,* 365 U.S. 43 (1961).
25. *Freedman v. Maryland,* 380 U.S. 51 (1965).
26. 383 U.S. 463 (1966).
27. *Mishkin v. New York,* 383 U.S. 502 (1966).

These two cases, however, represent an aberration in the long-term trend toward liberalization of the restrictions on sexual expression. Not once in the years prior to 1966 had the Supreme Court declared a specific work to be obscene; for all practical purposes, judicial policy-making had been a one-way street.

Although the thrust of the Court's decisions is manifest, the norms and concepts which emerged are broad and ambiguous. The Court has done little to refine substantive doctrines (e.g., what *kind* of social value is redeeming?) nor has it provided common-sense translations of its amorphous terminology (e.g., what *is* prurience?). Even if it is assumed that the Court subscribes to the theory under which "hard-core pornography" exhausts the category of the constitutionally obscene,[28] much doubt lingers about the sum and substance of this class of materials. If obscenity embraces *more* than the kind of speech connoted by the hard-core, then, *a fortiori,* the problems of applying the Supreme Court's doctrines to specific cases are exacerbated.

A significant implication of this ambiguity is the enormous discretion which has devolved on state appellate courts as they apply the constitutional guidelines furnished by the High Court. Acting consistently with their subordinate status within the federal system, the state courts have been relatively free to create public policy and infuse their own values into the law. Indeed, the generally accepted duty of rendering independent judgement on the constitutionality of disputed publications has impelled the courts in many states to declare themselves on the issue of sex expression.

A brief comparison of two appellate courts at opposite ends of the policy spectrum illustrates the variance in judicial approaches to obscenity cases. The Maryland Court of Appeals, by ruling in favor of sexual speech in ten out of twelve obscenity cases handled in the last decade, has seriously obstructed the state's motion picture censorship operation. Among the films approved are: *This Picture Is*

28. This interpretation was advanced by the Supreme Court's oblique equation in *Redrup v. New York,* 386 U.S. 767, 770 (1967), of the hard-core standard with the "not dissimilar" three-sided test articulated by the Court in *Memoirs v. Massachusetts,* 383 U.S. 413 (1966). The "three sides" are prurient interest, patent offensiveness, and social value.

Censored, consisting of "provocative" clips from banned films; [29] *Dirty Girls;* [30] and *Lorna,* which contains implied scenes of sexual intercourse.[31] Other media have also fared well in the "Free State": convictions for the sale of *Tropic of Cancer* were upset prior to the book's legitimation by the United States Supreme Court; [32] packets of photographs comprising sequential strip tease acts have been sanctioned.[33] The doctrines accompanying these decisions have also been permissive; for example, the Court ruled in *Yudkin v. State* [34] that the trial court is required to admit expert evidence when deciding issues of contemporary community standards and social value.

The *modus operandus* of the Maryland Court of Appeals is antithetical to the behavior of the Florida appellate courts which have endorsed lower court findings of obscenity in six out of eight cases decided in recent years. Among the works condemned by the highest tribunals in Florida have been *Tropic of Cancer,*[35] *Pleasure Is My Business,*[36] several "girlie" magazines including *Shape, Sizzle,* and *Harem,*[37] and *Miami Life,* a newspaper in which sexual relations between Negroes and whites are described.[38] In *Rachleff v. Mahon,* the hard-core pornography theory was explicitly rejected and obscenity was said to cover any "presentation and exploitation of illicit sex . . . passion, depravity, or immorality." [39]

If lower courts actually do adhere to the directives of superordinate

29. *Hewitt v. Maryland Board of Censors,* 241 Md. 283, 216 A.2d 557 (1966). The Maryland Court's stoic orientation toward obscenity is manifested in its assessment of *This Picture Is Censored:*

> While there is a most generous display of the female epidermis, both fore and aft, the whole thing is about as titillating and exciting as a ton of coal.

216 A.2d 557 (1966).
30. *Leighton v. Maryland Board of Censors,* 242 Md. 705, 218 A.2d 179 (1966).
31. *Dunn v. Maryland Board of Censors,* 240 Md. 249, 213 A.2d 751 (1965).
32. *Yudkin v. State,* 229 Md. 223, 182 A.2d 798 (1962).
33. *Monfred v. State,* 226 Md. 312, 173 A.2d 173 (1961).
34. 229 Md. 223, 182 A.2d 798 (1962).
35. *Grove Press v. Gerstein,* Fla., 151 So.2d 19 (1963), rev'd 378 U.S. 577 (1964).
36. *Tralins v. Gerstein,* Fla., 151 So.2d 19 (1963), rev'd 378 U.S. 576 (1964).
37. *Rachleff v. Mahon,* Fla., 124 So.2d 878 (1960).
38. *State v. Clein,* Fla., 93 So.2d. 876 (1957).
39. Fla., 124 So.2d 878, 882 (1960).

courts and if local elites (e.g., mayors, prosecutors, police chiefs) do pay heed to judicial policies, then booksellers located in states in which appellate courts have been permissive in their handling of obscenity cases should be more permissive in stocking, promoting, and selling sex literature than booksellers situated in states where higher court have been restrictive. Where the courts have fluctuated in their decision-making, bookseller behavior should fall midway on the self-censorship continuum.

THE EFFECT OF PUBLIC OPINION

Social pressures to conform to accepted norms can deter free expression just as rigorously as politico-legal restraints. Large-scale mass intolerance can overwhelm the palliative checking actions of courts, while public permissiveness can turn the anti-libertarian efforts of zealous officials into futile gestures ignored by society. Notwithstanding the oft-noted disparity between public opinion and social behavior, the public can set the gross limits of permissible expression. Furthermore, given the persistent and pervasive populist tendency in American social life,[40] "vox populi, vox Dei" is a force not to be ignored in an examination of censorship in the United States.

Public opinion can be conceptualized as the aggregate of individual attitudes on an issue of social policy. If a community is composed largely of persons with permissive attitudes toward sexual speech, the thresholds of public tolerance for sexual candor and crudity should be higher and social restraints imposed on booksellers should be fewer. Since an individual's attitudes on civil liberties issues are apparently related to his objective social characteristics,[41] the general

40. Daniel Bell, "The Dispossessed—1962," in Daniel Bell (ed.), *The Radical Right* (New York: Doubleday, 1963), p. 31.

41. The author analyzed two sets of data to show that well-established social determinants of intolerance are somewhat related to the issue of sex censorship. Urbanism, wealth, and education are statistically related to county voting behavior on the California anti-obscenity initiative of 1966 ("Proposition 16") while individual attitudes toward restrictions on sexual speech, as inferred from national survey data, are affected by urbanism, age, and physical mobility. See James Levine, "The Bookseller and the Law of Obscenity: Toward an Empirical Theory of Free Expression" (Unpublished Ph.D. dissertation, Department of Political Science, Northwestern University, 1968), chap. 4.

parameters of public opinion can be estimated by analyzing the demographic composition of a community.

In particular, the diversity of people, behavior, ideas, and values found in urban areas should be conducive to an atmosphere of public tolerance and sophistication, while the simplicity of small-town social structures and the homogeneity of rural populations should have the opposite effect of fostering intense negative public reactions to deviant expression. Also, public intolerance and bookseller self-censorship should be directly related to aggregate age levels within communities and inversely related to composite measures of education, wealth, and physical mobility.

THE BOOKSELLER SURVEY: METHODOLOGY AND FINDINGS

The data on self-censorship was obtained from a mail questionnaire returned by 63 per cent of a random sample of 250 booksellers in 12 states. Three categories of appellate court treatment of obscenity were represented as follows:

> permissive policies: California, Maryland, Oregon, and Pennsylvania
> fluctuating policies: Connecticut, Illinois, Massachusetts, Wisconsin
> restrictive policies: Florida, Missouri, New York, Ohio

The classification was made on the basis of a systematic scrutiny and analysis of all discoverable obscenity decisions of the highest courts of all fifty states over the last twenty years.[42]

By comparing the way in which different species of sex expression (e.g., "girlie" magazines, "art" films, sado-masochistic novels) were treated by different courts, it was possible to attain a reasonably detached and unbiased impression of the approach courts were taking in handling obscenity cases. Indeed, certain works, such as Henry Miller's *Tropic of Cancer* and John Cleland's *Fanny Hill,* were adjudicated in several jurisdictions prior to their appraisal by the United States Supreme Court. These decisions were particularly

42. Several categories of the "key" system of case indexing prepared by the West Publishing Company were searched to derive a complete list of obscenity cases, but it is entirely conceivable that some cases went unnoticed because they were catalogued in a legal rubric not scanned by this researcher.

useful in classifying courts, because they enabled us to observe variance in judicial output while controlling for the facts at issue.[43]

The criteria utilized to rank courts were twofold: (1) what the courts *said*, i.e., the severity or laxity of the rules of law enunciated, and (2) what the courts *did*, i.e., how frequently they ruled for or against sexual speech on trial. So that policies on obscenity could be isolated from judicial orientations toward other civil liberties questions, cases were weighted less heavily where the court refrained from evaluating the contents of specific works and grounded its judgement on issues of law enforcement procedure or the constitutionality of a statute on its face.

For both theoretical and practical reasons, the survey was restricted to dealers who are presumably "reputable," i.e., those who are making a *bona fide* effort to stay within the confines of the law of obscenity. Booksellers were randomly selected from the 1965 edition of the biennially revised *American Book Trade Directory* [44] which was the most authoritative source of active book dealers.

The questionnaire was intended to find the openness of the routine, day-to-day retail trade in books. A self-censorship scale was constructed by summating the responses to a series of "forced-choice" questions concerning book selection, sales, and promotion procedures. The following are a sample of the items incorporated into the scale:

> If a book has a reputation for being "controversial" due to its "realistic" or "shocking" portrait of sex, do you make a special effort to acquaint yourself with its contents?
>
> If a book contains frequent use of vulgar and profane language, does this in itself ever deter you from selecting the book for your store?
>
> Does your store generally refrain from selling books in which the central themes center on sexual perversion of one sort or another?
>
> Would you refrain from stocking a book that has a sexually seductive or erotic cover (e.g., a picture of a barely clad woman), even if you are certain that the contents of the book are not obscene?

43. No attempts were made to control for differences in statutory language among the twelve states. It was assumed that verbal variation in obscenity laws are inconsequential when courts are faced with the chore of deciding the constitutionality of suppressing particular works.
44. Eleanor Steiner-Prag, *American Book Trade Directory*, (New York: R. R. Bowker Co.; 17th ed., 1965).

Also included in the self-censorship scale were a series of items asking whether respondents stocked ten "sex books," ranging from the literary classic *Catcher in the Rye* (in which the word "fuck" is used incidentally) to *Fanny Hill*, which John Ciardi of the *Saturday Review* has called unmistakable pornography.[45]

At the permissive end of the scale fell booksellers who refrained from censorship and made available, candidly and unabashedly, a wide variety of publications dealing with sexual behavior or using profane language. At the other extreme, book dealers who systematically exclude sexually oriented materials from their inventories were considered to be restrictive.

The survey is inconclusive about the impact of legal norms of obscenity on bookseller behavior. Only 3 per cent of all respondents seek legal advice about the sale of books about sex on more than isolated occasions. More than half (57 per cent) acknowledged that they were unfamiliar with the specific provisions of local statutes and ordinances. Of even more significance is Table 1 which shows that only a small minority of booksellers are enlightened about the supposedly momentous decisions of the United States Supreme Court.

The wide abyss between judicial pronouncements and social responses can be observed by examining the short-run effects of *Ginzburg v. United States*,[46] the restrictive obscenity decision of 1966. Despite the extensive publicity and commentary which the case received in both mass media and professional journals, it failed to live up to its expectation as a harbinger of ill tidings for the retail bookseller. Although almost a full year had elapsed between the decision and the study, only 5 per cent of the entire sample consciously instigated any changes in their policies and practices as a direct result of *Ginzburg* and none of the modifications that were reported seemed to be major in scope. The Supreme Court may have donated a wealth of raw materials for the benefit of legal scholars, but its influence on the dissemination of sex literature in the general bookstore has been miniscule.

The hypothesis concerning the impact of state appellate courts was not confirmed by the data. Although Table 2 indicates that book-

45. John Ciardi, "What Is Pornography?" *Saturday Review*, July 13, 1963, p. 20.
46. 383 U.S. 463 (1966).

Table 1

BOOKSELLERS' KNOWLEDGE OF SUPREME COURT DECISIONS

Booksellers' General Awareness of Supreme Court Decisions [a]		Booksellers' Knowledge of *Roth v. United States* [b]	
I follow them very carefully.	15%	I am very familiar with the doctrines.	10%
I try to note the general trend in the law which they represent.	60	I know the major points made by the Court.	16
I don't follow them very much.	25	I have heard of the case, but don't know many details.	32
	100%	I am not familiar with the case.	42
Number of Cases	144		100%
		Number of Cases	144

[a] Item: How closely do you follow the decisions and opinions of the United States Supreme Court in the field of obscenity?

[b] Item: How familiar are you with the constitutional doctrines expressed by the United States Supreme Court in *Roth v. United States,* an obscenity case handed down in 1957?

Table 2

RELATION OF STATE APPELLATE COURT POLICY-MAKING TO NUMBER OF SEX BOOKS STOCKED [a] AND BOOKSELLER SELF-CENSORSHIP PRACTICES [b]

Number of Sex Books Stocked	Judicial Policy-Making			Self-Censorship Practices	Judicial Policy-Making		
	Restrictive	Fluctuating	Permissive		Restrictive	Fluctuating	Permissive
0–3	25%	35%	17%	Restrictive	34%	54%	25%
4–7	22	40	21	Moderate	32	27	31
8–10	53	25	61	Permissive	34	19	44
	100%	100%	99% [c]		100%	100%	100%
Number of Cases	55	40	47	Number of Cases	56	41	58

[a] Gamma = .10, not significant.

[b] Gamma = .10, not significant.

[c] Does not sum to 100 per cent because of rounding.

stores in permissive jurisdictions are slightly more lenient about peddling sex books than those in restrictive states, the percentage differences are so small that they could easily have resulted from mere chance. Booksellers governed by fluctuating courts, instead of exercising moderate censorship, turn out to be most restrictive of all. Because states in the "middle-of-the-road" category of judicial policy-making are out of expected alignment and the distributions of the two "extreme" classes of states do not differ radically, the rank-order correlations between judicial behavior and bookseller behavior are statistically insignificant.

It is conceivable that the anarchic patterns of Table 2 are artifacts of a faulty research methodology. The original respondent selection process may be responsible: if the three classes of states were not "matched" according to essential characteristics (such as the distribution of types of communities), the effects of judicial behavior are "contaminated" by extraneous variance. Also, the coding of appellate courts may have been unreliable, with the final court classification being more a figment of the researcher's imagination than a product of real differences.

On the other hand, theoretical conceptions may have been erroneous. The lines of communications connecting appellate courts, trial courts, political elites and booksellers may be so tenuous and haphazard that policy messages emanating from state capitols either become garbled or peter out entirely before reaching the local bookstall. Even if judicial dictates are successfully transmitted, they may be disregarded by local judges, police, prosecutors and merchants.

Whatever the reason, most respondents appeared to be unaffected by the policy-making of the state courts. Although 70 per cent of the sample answered affirmatively when asked if they usually find out about state and local court rulings on obscenity, these decisions are probably misunderstood or ignored.[47] From an academic point of view, the state judiciary plays a major role in the development and articulation of obscenity law, but the effect of the state courts on the censorship practices of the general bookseller is yet to be established.

---

47. The percentage probably overstates the extent of bookseller enlightenment because many of the responses may have been colored by a desire to appear knowledgeable and sophisticated. Others who claimed that they were aware of most judicial rulings may have been honestly mistaken.

Community characteristics also fail to explain a large part of the variance in bookseller behavior. The most powerful predictor is urbanism, and Table 3 indicates that aggregate population is indeed related to differences in censorship activity. It is quite clear that the bookstores located in large cities stock more "sex books" than their counterparts in smaller cities. However, the relationship between city size and self-censorship practices, barely significant statistically at the .10 level, is considerably weaker.

Table 3

RELATION OF COMMUNITY POPULATION TO NUMBER OF SEX BOOKS
STOCKED [a] AND BOOKSELLER SELF-CENSORSHIP PRACTICES [b]

Number of Sex Books Stocked	Population [c]			Self-Censorship Practices	Population [c]		
	Under 25,000	25,000– 249,999	250,000 and Over		Under 25,000	25,000– 249,999	250,000 and Over
0–3	31%	28%	16%	Restrictive	37%	44%	25%
4–7	33	27	21	Moderate	37	20	39
8–10	36	45	63	Permissive	25	36	36
	100%	100%	100%		99% [d]	100%	100%
Number of cases	39	60	43	Number of cases	40	61	44

[a] Gamma = .27, significant at the .01 level (one-tailed).
[b] Gamma = .14, significant at the .10 level (one-tailed).
[c] Population data are taken from the 1960 census.

In order to rebut the urbanism hypothesis, one might contend that more sex books are stocked in large cities *only because* of greater consumer demand. According to this argument, the low correlation between population and self-censorship practices is *more* significant in that it is based on questions about activities intended to be censorial in nature. Acts of commission would be deemed more important than acts of omission.

A rejoinder is available. First, booksellers can actively manipulate demand curves through their merchandising policies, and the reader's freedom is really dependent on the willingness of retailers to expose customers to a broad range of literary matter. Second, responses to questions about specific books may be a more reliable indicator of self-censorship because booksellers have an identical frame of reference and little room is left for subjective interpretation. Finally, because a book is either stocked or not stocked, unless a bookseller lies outright, it is more difficult for him to falsify his position in an attempt to project either a Comstockian or libertarian image.

Population density, another component of urbanism, is more strongly correlated with marketing practices, as is evidenced by Table 4. This tends to confirm the hypothesis suggested by Louis

Table 4

RELATION OF POPULATION DENSITY OF COMMUNITIES TO NUMBER OF
SEX BOOKS STOCKED [a] AND BOOKSELLER SELF-CENSORSHIP PRACTICES [b]

Number of Sex Books Stocked	Population Density [c]			Self-Censorship Practices	Population Density [c]		
	Low	Medium	High		Low	Medium	High
0–3	36%	21%	17%	Restrictive	56%	36%	25%
4–7	23	29	22	Moderate	17	31	32
8–10	41	50	60	Permissive	26	32	42
	100%	100%	99% [d]		99% [d]	99% [d]	99% [d]
Number of cases	22	38	40	Number of cases	23	39	40

[a] Gamma = .24, significant at the .05 level (one-tailed).
[b] Gamma = .29, significant at the .05 level (one-tailed).
[c] Population density is taken from the 1960 census and is measured in terms of population per square mile.
[d] Does not sum to 100 per cent due to rounding.

Wirth that density "reinforces the effects of numbers by diversifying men and their activities and increasing the complexity of the social structure." [48] Concentration of large numbers of people into relatively small physical spaces such as apartment buildings apparently conduces public tolerance by increasing exposure to variegated stimuli and necessitating, in the interest of social harmony, an "each-to-his-own" attitude among residents.

48. Louis Wirth, "Urbanism as a Way of Life," in Albert Reiss (ed.), *On Cities and Social Life* (Chicago: University of Chicago Press, 1964), p. 73.

Many respondents in small communities explained and defended their restrictiveness by referring to the necessity of respecting community mores so as to maintain a good reputation among the public. The remarks of a Maryland bookseller reveal the powerful regulative effects of social custom in settings involving relatively limited numbers of people:

> We are a modest store in a moderately sized city. Many of our customers are, or have become, friends. We have tried to build a store which would reflect ourselves as persons, through the atmosphere of the store, our personnel, and the kind of services we offer, as well as the books we sell. We do our own censoring, but primarily we take our standards from those of the community. This policy has worked very well for us.

Nevertheless, when the low correlations between urbanism and bookseller behavior are taken in conjunction with the even smaller relationships detected between self-censorship and other demographic variables, there is ample cause for skepticism about the supposed connection between public sentiment toward freedom and actual curtailment of civil liberties. Of course, it is possible that gross census data on community structure (e.g., median income) is too broad-gauged of a measure to permit inferences about community opinion. It may have been erroneous or misleading to use entire cities as relevant communities (as was done in the present study) when public opinion within smaller social units, such as the neighborhood, may have a greater effect on bookseller behavior. However, the null hypothesis may be correct: what the public thinks, feels, fears, and dislikes may have little bearing on the kinds of literature available in the open market.

The meager findings reported above are in stark contrast to the strong positive relationship between booksellers' personal attitudes toward obscenity and their self-censorship practices. Booksellers' attitudes were determined from a series of questions about the desirability of sex censorship, and Table 5 convincingly demonstrates that variance in censorship behavior is explicable in terms of respondents' psychological predispositions on this social issue.

The rank-order correlations of .80 and .78 practically speak for themselves, and the almost symmetrical matrices of Table 5 attest to

Table 5

RELATION OF BOOKSELLERS' ATTITUDES TOWARD SEXUAL SPEECH TO
NUMBER OF SEX BOOKS STOCKED [a] AND SELF-CENSORSHIP PRACTICES [b]

| | Booksellers' Attitudes | | | | Booksellers' Attitudes | | |
Number of Sex Books Stocked	Restrictive	Moderate	Permissive	Self-Censorship Practices	Restrictive	Moderate	Permissive
0–3	52%	24%	0%	Restrictive	72%	29%	4%
4–7	36	31	12	Moderate	18	48	29
8–10	11	45	88	Permissive	9	24	67
	99% [c]	100%	100%		99% [c]	101% [c]	100%
Number of cases	52	42	49	Number of cases	54	42	49

[a] Gamma = .80, significant at the .001 level (one-tailed).
[b] Gamma = .78, significant at the .001 level (one-tailed).
[c] Does not sum to 100 per cent due to rounding.

a convergence of attitudes and behavior. Booksellers who find coarse or detailed discussions of sex personally repugnant are likely to avoid handling this kind of merchandise, restricting their inventory to books which are reticent about sex. Conversely, dealers who welcome, or at least condone, explicit portrayals of sexual conduct are more willing to carry books about sex which are shocking and repulsive to large segments of the society.

Although legitimate questions could be raised about the validity of the attitude measure, the quantitative analysis is complemented by the written remarks offered by booksellers. A fascinating consistency can be discovered between the degree of censorship exercised and the "temper" and emphasis of respondents' discourses on the subjects of censorship and obscenity. For example, a permissive Wisconsin bookseller replied as follows:

> Obscenity . . . is not a large problem today. After all, we have minds and can pick and choose what we wish to put into them. The so-called blunt or obscene language used in many books are in all cases tame compared to the vocabulary of most people, whether "high or low born." So personally, I cannot find reason to condemn a book on that basis. Keep them from children, yes, but adults should be able to pick and choose as they will. After all, who wants

to be their "brother's keeper" all the time or even is capable of the task.

A quite different tone is conveyed by the words of a Pennsylvania respondent who imposes rigorous censorship controls:

> They tell me *The Arrangement* which shocked me isn't any worse than the *Valley of the Dolls*. I didn't even read the first pages of that, but since it held the bestseller top place so long it probably was sexy. I wouldn't know—a good *clean* murder story for me!

The role perceptions of booksellers also affect their marketing practices. Where booksellers visualized their social positions as civic leaders, protectors of children, or guardians of public morals, it is not surprising to discover that they eschew "racy" literature. Contrariwise, booksellers who perceive themselves as merchants, pure and simple, often suppress their personal feelings about obscenity because of their preoccupation with the attainment of financial profits. The words of a Massachusetts respondent bespeak a businessman's plea more than a libertarian's credo:

> I run a bookstore; it's my only living. I sell only what the public buys. In my store, you can buy a crossword puzzle book, a Bible, Shakespeare, *Fanny Hill, Candy,* etc. If outsiders want to run my store, I'll give them the key and they can send me my pay and sell whatever they want. Remember, you can only sell what people want to buy.

The data compellingly intimate that *internal psychological forces* impinging on booksellers, be they attitudes or role perceptions, are primary causes of freedom and censorship in the general bookstore. This was surmised over a decade ago by Eric Larrabee:

> Of all the forms of sex censorship, that of the individual psyche —which sees to it that some things cannot be said, even to oneself— is undoubtedly the most effective.[49]

To a great extent, public access to books about sex is dependent upon the open-mindedness and the moral irresponsibility of individuals who comprise the bookselling profession.

49. Eric Larrabee, "The Cultural Context of Sex Censorship," *Law and Contemporary Problems,* 20 (Autumn 1955), p. 673.

CONCLUSION

In the domain of sex censorship, "what is obscene?" has been called the "core constitutional question," [50] and in the literary realm of communications, it is the bookseller, rather than the courts or the masses, who provides the most definitive and relevant answer. This suggests that individuals who occupy social positions enabling them to screen public speech may possess considerable autonomy in controlling the range of freedom permitted in a society. Since judicial behavior and community demography were poor predictors of censorship in the bookstore and since booksellers' attitudes correlated highly with their censorship behavior, it may well be that neither legal nor social forces can easily pierce the inner shell of personal prejudices, preferences, and inhibitions which seem to motivate those who function as "gatekeepers" of public speech. The courts may command and the public may opine, but the bookseller is, by and large, the master of his own fate.

If these limited findings can be extrapolated to other social situations having civil liberties dimensions, then some of our *a priori* notions about the empirical roots of freedom may need overhauling. The external forces of constitutional law and public opinion may actually be less significant and influential than the internal moralities and attitude structures of the corps of elites and sub-elites who, like the bookseller, allocate freedom to the society.

50. William Lockhart and Robert McClure, "Obscenity Censorship: The Core Constitutional Question—What Is Obscene?" *Utah Law Review*, 7 (Spring 1961), p. 289.

MICHAEL S. WALD, ET AL.

Interrogations in New Haven: The Impact of Miranda

INTRODUCTION

The Supreme Court decision in *Miranda v. Arizona* has been a touchstone of debate over the rules protecting the rights of suspects. The debate, begun even before *Miranda*, ranges from courts to police academies, from law reviews to popular magazines. Myriad claims regarding the likely impact of the ruling on law enforcement and "crime in the streets," are bandied about. Although the controversy has been singularly lacking in facts to support any position,[1] some critics of the decision are sufficiently upset to recommend a constitutional amendment reversing the decision.

Impressed by the need for systematic answers to the questions and claims cast up by the controversy, we undertook a study of the implementation and effect of *Miranda*. The core of the effort involved stationing observers at the New Haven, Connecticut, police headquarters around the clock for an eleven-week period during the summer of 1966. These observers witnessed all the interrogations conducted by the police during this period. In addition to the obser-

1. This has been recognized by many of the participants in the controversy. *See, e.g.*, Brief for New York as Amicus Curiae at 21-24, Miranda v. Arizona, 384 U.S. 436 (1966). *See also Developments in the Law—Confessions*, 79 HARV. L. REV. 935, 945 (1966), opining, characteristically, that the factual questions are "unanswered and perhaps unanswerable."

From *The Yale Law Journal*, 76, pp. 1521–1648. Reprinted by permission of the Yale Law Journal Company, Fred B. Rothman & Company, and the authors.

The authors were editors of *The Yale Law Journal* in 1966–1967. The project editor, Michael S. Wald, is now Assistant Professor of Law at Stanford School of Law.

vations, interviews provided additional data for our study of the likely impact of *Miranda,* supplying the perspectives of the various participants in the criminal process—the detectives, prosecutors, defense lawyers, and suspects themselves.

The project attempts, essentially, to evaluate the claims that interrogations are inherently coercive and that *Miranda* will substantially impede successful law enforcement.[2] Four general questions are explored: What is the interrogation process like? What has been the impact of *Miranda* on the suspect's willingness to cooperate? How important are interrogations for successful solution of crime? Finally, what would be the impact of a lawyer in the stationhouse? The practical problems of implementing the decision are explored only briefly. No attempt is made to defend or attack the value judgements underlying the positions involved.[3] For some people, our approach is probably irrelevant, although, we hope, interesting. *Miranda* can be supported without any knowledge of the potentially adverse effects of the decision: some commentators argue that the constitutional bar

2. The decision raises questions about the constitutional basis of the holding, the competence of the Court for such specific rule-making, the values underlying the decision, the effects the decision will have on law enforcement, and the problems of implementation.

The approach of this study is directed to the positions taken by those critics and supporters of the decision whose arguments are based on factual issues, since these are the only testable ones. While supporters of *Miranda* rely primarily on constitutional and value arguments, they also claim that interrogations are coercive and unnecessary. *See* 384 U.S. at 436-60; N. SOBEL, THE NEW CONFESSION STANDARDS (1966).

The critics claim *Miranda* will severely hamper law enforcement. This position is set forth in the brief for government in Westover v. United States, 384 U.S. 436 (1966), at 17: "We start from the premise that it is essential to the protection of society that law-enforcement officials be permitted to interrogate an arrested suspect." It was adopted by the dissenters in *Miranda:* "There is every . . . reason to believe that a good many criminal defendants who otherwise would have been convicted . . . will now . . . either not be tried at all or will be acquitted . . . ." 384 U.S. at 542 (dissenting opinion of White, J.). This position has been advocated by many commentators.

3. Various value positions underlie the claims of both critics and supporters. For example, the supporters claim interrogations without warnings threaten human dignity and that a system without such safeguards is unjust. The critics, on the other hand, assert that law-abiding citizens are the primary people about whom to be concerned and that they should not be denied protection in order to safeguard rights of "known" criminals.

against compulsory self-incrimination is absolute and decisive;[4] others contend that to promote overall justice in the criminal process we must provide warnings to suspects, regardless of impact.[5] However, most critics and supporters alike rely on factual as well as value positions. This study attempts to provide some data for their discussion.

* * *

Changes in Police Behavior

To test whether our presence substantially affected police behavior, we tried to find out how the police acted before and after our observations. We interviewed 40 persons who had been interrogated during the four months preceding and following our three-month study.[6] We asked them to describe the same features of their interrogations that our observers recorded in the police station. Assuming that the process might be perceived differently from the suspect's perspective, we also interviewed 20 of the people whom we saw questioned last summer. By asking them questions to which we already had answers, we could tell how much, and on what points, their reports differed from those of our observers. This factor could then be applied to the interviews with the other suspects to estimate how accurate their reports were likely to be.[7]

4. This position is inherent in the majority opinion in *Miranda* 479. *See also* E. GRISWOLD, THE FIFTH AMENDMENT TODAY 75 (1955).

5. Weisberg, *Police Interrogation of Arrested Persons: A Skeptical View*, in POLICE POWER AND INDIVIDUAL FREEDOM 153, 179-80 (C. Sowle, ed., 1962).

6. We had hoped to be able to interview a larger number of suspects. Unfortunately, we were denied access to the state prison and reformatories and this limited our sample to those people in jail or on probation. Many of those that were on probation were hard to find. It was not until we obtained the services of a former convict, now working for the Legal Assistance Association, that we were able to locate any defendants whatsoever. Fortunately, a number of those interviewed had been arrested several times over the past five years so we were able to get a comparison over a fairly long period.

7. This is, of course, a crude test. However, since the test indicated there was no significant change, problems with the test do not affect the validity of the findings.

Almost half of the interviewed suspects whom we had observed described their interrogations differently than our observer. The discrepancies followed no pattern; some even reported the process more favorably, saying, for example, they had received *Miranda* warnings when our observer had not recorded any such warnings. However, most respondents reported a more hostile interrogation than our observer recorded. Two suspects reported falsely that they were hit at the Detective Division. From this evidence, it seems probable that the responses of the people questioned before and after our observation period were also somewhat inaccurate.

Yet, even if we do not assume any exaggeration by the groups we did not observe, their description of the process was so similar to what we did observe that we feel justified in assuming our presence did not markedly affect the detectives' behavior.[8] If there were any changes, they appear to have been in the interrogation tactics used by the police. As we discuss below, during the summer the atmosphere at interrogations seemed generally friendly or businesslike to our observers; the police employed very few tactics such as threats, promises or trickery. From the reports of those we interviewed it appears that the detectives frequently displayed a more hostile air before and after our months of observation. The police told suspects more often that they would be "worse off" if they did not talk, played down the seriousness of the crime, swore at the suspects, and made promises of leniency. However, last summer we did find such tactics used frequently in the cases which the police considered most serious. The large proportion of serious crimes in the unobserved sample may therefore account for the more frequent use of such tactics.

Our belief that our presence had but slight effect is further supported by the impressions of our observers. Initially, our presence

8. From these interviews we learned that interrogations had been conducted in the same rooms throughout. Almost all interrogations were about the same length as our summer average. No suspect indicated he had been denied a lawyer, either before or after *Miranda*, although a number of post-*Miranda* suspects indicated no warnings had been given them. This was also true during the summer. Even before *Miranda* most suspects were allowed to call friends and relatives, and were offered cigarettes and food. Only six of the people reported they had been treated badly; the others said their treatment was "o.k."

was viewed skeptically. The detectives treated us with suspicion, greeted us by silence, and locked the observers out of the detective headquarters when they left. Within two weeks, however, the attitudes of the detectives had changed markedly. They became friendly with the observers, talked and joked freely, and gave us free run of the station. The people on the night shift particularly seemed to enjoy having someone to talk with.

Aside from their apparently unguarded behavior, several other factors suggest that the police acted naturally after the first few weeks. The detectives frequently did not follow the letter of the law, and often gave no warnings despite our presence. As the summer progressed they also became more candid in their conversations. They tried, for instance, to justify, not to hide, their various prejudices.[9] Some detectives also admitted that coercive interrogations were sometimes useful, though this was invariably qualified—"of course, it doesn't happen any more."[10]

*   *   *

ADHERENCE TO LEGAL NORMS

Physical Coercion

We saw no undue physical force used by the detectives.[11] From what we sensed about the attitudes of the detectives in both divisions, we

9. Almost all of the detectives were extremely biased against Negroes. However, this bias, while often voiced, was seldom evidenced during interrogations.
10. For a similar conclusion for a different police department see J. SKOLNICK, JUSTICE WITHOUT TRIAL 36 (1966). Skolnick's presence was less likely to affect behavior since he was with the police only sporadically.
11. At the Detective Division the policemen sometimes were forced to subdue an unruly suspect, but this was accomplished without relish. None of the detectives ever threatened violence overtly, though a few appeared threatening whenever they lost their tempers. We were not present in the police cars between the time suspects were arrested and when they arrived at the Detective Division headquarters, but there was no evidence that they were taken elsewhere for questioning or that they were physically abused before being brought to the station.

doubt that many of them would employ force as a calculated tool to pry out a confession.[12]

In the first place, neither division often needs a confession badly enough to beat someone up for it, because both usually have so much evidence when they arrest suspects and because the crimes are not generally very serious. Second, few of the detectives are calculating or ruthless in their attempts to extract a confession. They find interrogating a challenging game in which they try hard to outwit the suspect. But few are such crusaders against crime that they feel physical violence is justified to get a confession.[13]

Giving Advice of Rights

According to the detectives, before *Miranda* suspects were advised that they might remain silent and that anything they said could be used against them.[14] The *Miranda* decision therefore meant that the detectives had only to include advice about counsel to fulfill the new requirements. The new rules were not adhered to in most of the cases we observed—nor were the old. Despite the presence of our observers in the police station, the detectives gave all the advice required by *Miranda* to only 25 of 118 suspects questioned. Nonetheless most suspects did receive some advice; only 22 per cent of the suspects were not advised at all of their constitutional rights. The most frequently given warning was the right to silence—90 of the suspects were told. While only 51 were advised that anything they might say could be used against them, 81 were told they had a right to counsel, but only 27 of their right to appointed counsel.

The detectives clearly gave more adequate advice later in the sum-

12. Of course, our presence may have affected their behavior. Several of the detectives in the Detective Division said that they had transferred from the Special Services Division because they "didn't like the way things were done over there." One candidly told an observer that he had left the Special Services Division because they used too much force on suspects. In one case during the summer, a Special Services detective used excessive force in arresting a woman suspect. Other isolated incidents of such conduct were disclosed to us through several conversations with detectives.

13. Special Services belies the generalization. In this division most of the detectives seemed to feel they were the protectors of the public against vice and morals offenders.

14. Our impressions during the two weeks of observation before *Miranda* were that suspects were rarely warned and never at the outset of questioning.

mer, however, as they became more accustomed to the *Miranda* requirements; much of the non-compliance may therefore have been transitional. (See Table 1.) During the two weeks of June after *Miranda* less than half the suspects received a warning which included more than half the elements of the *Miranda* advice,[15] but by August more than two-thirds of the suspects received such a warning. More important, the number of full *Miranda* statements increased even more dramatically. No suspects received the full *Miranda* statement in June, while more than one-third of those questioned in August received the complete warning.

Table 1

ADVICE OF RIGHTS, BY MONTH, FOR ALL INTERROGATIONS [16]

| | Month | | | |
Advice of Rights	June	July	August	Total
0–2 warnings	14	31	14	59
3–4 warnings	9	22	28	49
Total	23	53	42	108
Full *Miranda* advice	0	8	17	

Not ascertained: 2
Not questioned: 9

Chi Square significant at .05 level.

Undoubtedly the detectives' initial failure to give the *Miranda* advice was partly attributable to ignorance. Although the detectives

15. The detectives may have had little chance to adjust to the *Miranda* decision in June.

16. In this table, as in others throughout the article, we will often divide the measure of the adequacy of the advice given the suspect into two categories. The category of less adequate warnings includes those in which the detective told the suspect nothing about his right, or gave him one or two parts of the four-part *Miranda* warning. In nearly every case in this category the detective advised the suspect of his right to silence and/or to counsel. The category of more adequate warnings includes those incorporating three or four parts of the *Miranda* advice. The usual three-part warnings included the statement that anything the suspect said could be used against him; the advice of the right to appointed counsel was almost never given unless all other parts of the *Miranda* warnings were also recited.

   The last figure on the chart shows the number of interrogations in which the detectives repeated all four parts of the *Miranda* advice of rights.

were told of the decision by their superiors, few of them seemed to understand its requirements. Only one of the line detectives, so far as we could tell, had read the decision by the time we left the station-house. Toward the end of the summer, those who took the depart-ment's in-service training course began to receive more complete lectures on *Miranda,* so that by the end of last year all the detectives should have known what advice of rights they were required to give. Near the end of the observation period, cards giving the *Miranda* advice were passed out by the department to all the detectives and patrolmen with instructions to read one to each suspect at arrest. At the same time all detectives were given a waiver-of-rights form which they were to have the suspect sign before they questioned him.[17]

These remarks must be qualified for the Special Services Division. There the detectives were more conscious of the letter of the pre-scribed advice soon after it was promulgated. Consequently, their omissions generally seemed to be intentional.[18]

Despite increasing adherence to the letter of *Miranda,* however, both groups of detectives complied less readily with its spirit. By and large the detectives regarded giving the suspect this advice an artifi-cial imposition on the natural flow of the interrogation—an imposition for which they could see little reason. Most incorporated into their tactical repertoire some sort of hedging on the warnings, when they were given. Some changed the warning slightly: "Whatever you say may be used *for* or against you in a court of law." Often, the detec-tives advised the suspect with some inconsistent qualifying remark, such as "You don't have to say a word, but you ought to get every-

17. The card read as follows:

WARNING

I am a Police Officer. I warn you that anything you say will be used in a Court of law against you; That you have an absolute right to remain silent; That you have the right to advice of a lawyer before and the presence of a lawyer here with you *during* questioning, and
That if you cannot afford a lawyer, one will be appointed for you free before any questioning if you desire.
18. The detective who had read the decision, and who seemed to understand most fully its implications, was a member of Special Services. Perhaps his knowledge was responsible for that of his comrades.

thing cleared up," or "You don't have to say anything, of course, *but* can you explain how . . . ." [19]

Even when the detective advised the suspect of his rights without these undercutting devices, he commonly de-fused the advice by implying that the suspect had better not exercise his rights,[20] or by delivering his statement in a formalized bureaucratic tone to indicate that his remarks were simply a routine, meaningless legalism. Instinctively, perhaps, the detectives heightened the unreality of the *Miranda* advice by emphasizing the formality of their statement. Often they would bring the flow of conversation to a halt and preface their remarks with, "Now I am going to warn you of your rights." After they had finished the advice they would solemnly intone, "Now you have been warned of your rights," then immediately shift to a conversational tone to ask, "Now, would you like to tell me what happened?"

In the few cases where a suspect showed an interest in finding a lawyer and did not already know one, the police usually managed to head him off simply by not helping him to locate one. Sometimes they refused to advise the suspect whether he should have a lawyer with him during questioning; more often they merely offered him a telephone book without further comment, and that was enough to deter him from calling a lawyer.

What circumstances influenced the detective's compliance with Miranda? Only one explanation for the varying compliance by the detectives—other than the change over time—survived statistical testing. For the sample as a whole, persons suspected of more serious crimes were given more adequate advice of their rights than those suspected of less serious crimes.[21] (See Table 2.) Our data showed

19. Sometimes the advice was not given until extensive questioning had occurred.

20. This was usually conveyed by tone or manner of delivery.

21. "Serious" is used here to denote the New Haven detectives' evaluation. To obtain the evaluation, each detective interviewed was given a stack of cards with crimes printed on them and asked to place each under one of four headings: Least Serious, Fairly Serious, Serious, and Most Serious. The average results provided a basis for ranking crimes on an ordinal scale from 1 to 4. "Ordinal" implies that we know only that category (2) is more serious than category (1), not how much more, and that the scale is not absolute. The latter point is important because New Haven has a relatively low rate of violent crimes against the person. On another scale some of the crimes ranked "Serious" by the detectives might appear relatively trivial.

Table 2

ADVICE OF RIGHTS, BY SERIOUSNESS OF CRIME, FOR ALL INTERROGATIONS

Advice of Rights	Seriousness of Crime		Total
	Less Serious	More Serious	
0–2 Warnings	36	21	57
3–4 Warnings	20	36	56
	56	57	113

Not ascertained: 5
Not questioned: 9

Chi Square significant at .01 level.

no statistical relationship between the availability of evidence and the giving of warnings. But if we look only at the 56 suspects accused of more serious crimes, our data suggest—although not to a statistically significant degree—an interesting and highly rational set of priorities for giving the advice of rights. (See Table 3.)

Table 3

ADVICE OF RIGHTS, BY EVIDENCE AVAILABLE, FOR SUSPECTS OF
SERIOUS CRIMES

Advice	Evidence			Total
	Enough To Convict	Enough for Trial	Not Enough for Trial	
0–2 Warnings	10	4	6	20
3–4 Warnings	14	14	8	36
	24	18	14	56

Not ascertained: 8
Not questioned: 9
Less serious crime: 54

Chi Square not significant at .05 level.

The suspect of a serious crime was most likely to get a more adequate warning in the cases where the police had enough evidence to go to trial, but not enough for a conviction. Thus, the police seemed most careful to insure the admissibility of the suspect's statement when they had a case against the suspect but when it was not clear that he could be convicted without an incriminating statement as evidence. The detectives apparently worried less about the admissibility of the statement if the case seemed open and shut. They were also apparently more willing, from sheer necessity, to take a chance on admissibility when they did not have enough evidence to get to trial unless the suspect incriminated himself.

This pattern is consistent with the conception of their job which many of the detectives seemed to hold. Perhaps as a result of past experience with the prosecutor's office, they often seemed to feel that their job was to produce some written evidence against the suspect and let the prosecutor handle the case after that. Given the detectives' rather narrow conception of their part in the criminal process, it would not be surprising to find them more interested in obtaining some kind of statement to present to the prosecutor than in the statement's admissibility at trial.

* * *

THE MOST COERCIVE INTERROGATIONS

Throughout the preceding discussion we have dealt with each aspect of psychological interrogation and adherence to legal norms in isolation, stressing the low level of coerciveness in most questioning. Here, we shall examine the 17 interrogations where the police put most of the elements of psychological interrogation together, isolated the suspect from friends, and disregarded his right to end questioning.

Although we shall call these interrogations "coercive," we should note at the outset that some of them might not be legally coercive under *Miranda* and past coerced-confession decisions.[22] In four of the cases the full *Miranda* warning was given, and the suspect was either allowed to terminate the interrogation or made no attempt to do so. The police used more than three tactics in 16 of the 17 interrogations, and many more in several of them. But under the traditional due

22. On the other hand, suspects in some of the cases not labeled coercive may have been legally coerced into confessing—*e.g.*, some with short interrogations were not given warnings.

process standard for coercion, probably few of these interrogations were coercive enough to invalidate the evidence elicited. For example, the police questioned only two of the 17 for as long as seven hours, and only eight for more than one hour. Even though the detectives' procedures in these interrogations were certainly less than a civil-libertarian's ideal, some of them would have been difficult to challenge successfully in court.

To isolate these interrogations, we used as many as possible of the indexes of interrogation techniques and adherence to legal norms discussed in the previous sections. We felt that we could not consider coercive the detective's failure to offer a suspect amenities. Rather, it was more likely to mean that the interrogation had been short, or that the detective had simply forgotten to make the offer. We also did not use the index of the detective's advice of rights, since we felt that inadequate advice was largely a function of the date of the interrogation.

Five indicators of a coercive interrogation were used: (1) whether the attitude of the police towards the suspect was "hostile" or "ambiguous"; [23] (2) whether the detectives employed three or more tactics; (3) whether they questioned the suspect for more than one hour; (4) whether they refused to stop questioning after the suspect indicated that he wanted to terminate the interrogation; [24] (5) whether they neglected to tell the suspect he could contact friends or family until after questioning was completed.[25] None of the interro-

23. The latter was included because of our feeling that the ambiguity arising from the use of contrasting adjectives to describe the detectives' conduct may have meant that the detectives had gone to considerable trouble to ensnare the suspect with a tactic.
24. We did not include the cases in which the suspect had made no attempt to terminate questioning, since in these cases the detective had not violated the rules of *Miranda*.
25. We did not include interrogations in which the detectives had simply not told the suspect at all that he could contact friends and family because of our feeling that the failure to mention the privilege was often a mere oversight on the part of the interrogator, or resulted from the brevity of the interrogation. Furthermore, we had noted that when the detectives apparently wanted to prevent the suspect from calling, but also wanted to say that he had been offered the chance to call, they generally advised him after the interrogation.
    The detectives virtually never denied a suspect amenities after he had requested them, so we could not use the denial of amenities as an indicator of coercion.
    Furthermore, we felt that amenities were sometimes offered, as well as with-

gations in our sample included all five of these indicators; only three interrogations included four of the five. We decided to examine closely the 17 interrogations wherein we found three or more of the indicators.[26] . . . [T]he detectives were hostile or ambiguous, and used three or more tactics, in most of the interrogations chosen by this method. The other three indicators were erratically distributed.[27]

---

held, to induce the suspect to talk, so that it was not clear in any given case what meaning could be attached to the fact that the detectives had not offered amenities. As it turned out, our feelings appear justified; 8 of the 17 suspects selected by the five indicators we used had been offered cigarettes.

26. One or more of these indicators was found in 85 of the 121 interrogations we had watched, but most interrogations included only one or two of them. The large number of interrogations in which one or two indicators of coercion appeared corroborated our earlier conclusion that the detectives employed these devices half-heartedly most of the time.

Our confidence in the value of the method of selecting the 17 interrogations for analysis was increased when we discovered that all seven of the interrogations from which the detectives tried to exclude us were selected by it.

27. One observer conveniently recorded, immediately after the interrogation, a conversation which formed one of these 17 interrogations. We repeat it here to give some of the flavor of the "most coercive" interrogations:

> Subject had been picked up at 5 A.M. Car 15 had gone up the street and patrolman had followed to give possible assistance. Subject and another youth came running down the street. Patrolman apprehended subject. Stolen car was then found parked on the street in front of subject's home. Subject was accused of having taken the car. Interrogation proceeded as follows:
>
> Detective: "It's pretty obvious you were in the stolen car. You were running away from it and from the policeman. Taking a car for a joyride [taking a car without owner's permission] is a lot less serious offense than car theft, so relatively what you did was a pretty minor offense. You were running away, we have you I'd say, so it'll go a lot easier for you if you just tell me now exactly what you did. You'll be charged with the lesser offense, and the judge will go easier with you if you say: 'I made a mistake and it won't happen again. . . .' Maybe you didn't even take the car, but were just a rider in it.
>
> If we have to put you on a lie detector, well, that would take a lot of time and expense, and we wouldn't be too happy about that.
>
> So, I'm being honest with you, and now I want you to be man enough to admit what you did. You don't have to tell me about the other guy, just yourself. Will you take a lie detector test?"
>
> Suspect claims he knows nothing. Detective's tone then gets tougher, aggravation enters his voice, and a few flares of temper. Indicates that he doubts the suspect's story. Calls the home of a girl the suspect says he was talking to at the time of the car theft—the line is busy. Threatens to confront the suspect with the girl or her mother. Gets the name of

INTERROGATIONS

Having isolated these interrogations, we tried to determine why the detectives had been more coercive in them. We found here, as in previous sections, that the detectives interrogated aggressively in serious crimes when they needed evidence to insure the suspect's conviction, when they needed the name of an accomplice, or when they felt the suspect could help them clear other crimes. In nine of the 17 interrogations, the police needed a confession or admission to assure conviction.

Five of the remaining eight were directed toward solving other crimes, primarily breaking-and-enterings. In the other three interrogations, we could find no reason for the use of coercion. In each the police had enough evidence to convict before questioning, and the questioning was directed only toward obtaining evidence against the suspect himself.

Almost all the suspects in these interrogations had been arrested for relatively serious crimes. Only five of the 17 crimes were among

---

the other kid who ran away from the police, threatens confrontation with him.

Detective: "If the other kid says the car was taken and you took it or were in it, I'll tell the judge how uncooperative you were. It'll be tough on you, and I'll try to give the other kid a break. (A moralistic tone enters his voice.) What were you doing out at 5 A.M. anyhow? We've got you, I'm certain, and you know it."

Then he locks the boy in the wire cage in the main room of the Detective Division. After a minute or two, he returns to the cage and talks to the subject. Buys him a soda. Subject says that only other kids were involved. Detective brings him to the fingerprint room to talk further. Subject says he was sitting on his porch, when the car drove up, some kids got out and ran off. When the patrol car came by, subject ran because he knew the police would pick up anyone around for questioning. Subject says he knows the kids—he gives the detective their first names. Detective says he doesn't want subject to be hurt by a record, so will keep subject out of it if subject's story is true. Will let subject go home if he agrees to come back at 12:30 P.M.

Subject doesn't appear at 12:30, and detective has only the first names of the other kids. Detective says he figures the subject fell asleep, and can always be picked up later. Detective believes him to be telling the truth.

those ranked "fairly serious" by the police; the other 12 were all among those ranked "serious" or "most serious."

We found no evidence that the police had used coercion in response to the personal characteristics of the suspects. Nor did they react to hostility from the suspects; in fact, this group of suspects was significantly more cooperative with the detectives than the sample as a whole. The proportion of Negroes and suspects with prior records was not significantly different from the sample as a whole. The 17 suspects were significantly younger than the sample as a whole; all were less than 30 years of age, and nine were less than 21. The large number of younger suspects, however, is probably accounted for by the fact that the crimes involved were more serious than those in the sample as a whole, since younger suspects tended to be arrested for more serious crimes.

The police gave noticeably more adequate advice of rights to these 17 suspects than to the sample as a whole. Eight of the 17 received the full four-part *Miranda* advice, one received three of the elements of the *Miranda* advice,[28] six received one or two of the elements,[29] and only two received no advice at all.

Despite the more adequate advice of rights given these suspects, the police were disproportionately successful in interrogating them. Seven of the suspects confessed; two admitted to their crimes; and two made incriminating statements. Only six of the 17 interrogations were unproductive. By comparison, only 21 suspects in the entire sample of 127 confessed, and only 11 made admissions.[30]

Surprisingly, the police were no less successful in the interrogations where they had given relatively adequate advice than in the others. Of the nine suspects given the full *Miranda* warning or three parts of it, four confessed, one made an admission, and another made an

28. Right to silence; right to counsel; anything he said could be used against him.
29. Usually right to silence and right to counsel, or right to silence alone.
30. Furthermore, some of the uncoerced confessions were virtually spontaneous. The police were not seriously interested in questioning two of the 14 suspects who made uncoerced confessions and three of the nine who made uncoerced admissions. Thus of all of the confessions and admissions which the police sought at all vigorously, one-third (nine of 27) occurred in the 17 coercive interrogations.

incriminating statement.[31] Similarly, three of the eight suspects given less adequate advice confessed; one made an admission; and one made an incriminating statement.

Our analysis of these 17 coercive interrogations thus indicates that the Court's fears of coerced confessions in *Miranda* are not groundless in New Haven, despite the lack of coercion in the typical interrogation. Aggressive interrogation pays off in confessions. Moreover, these cases suggest that the *Miranda* advice of rights does not reduce the value of coercion in obtaining confessions.

* * *

31. Although the other three gave no statement, it is not clear that the interrogations were failures. All three were co-suspects with one of those who confessed after being given the full *Miranda* advice. As soon as one of the four confessed, incriminating the other three, the police stopped questioning them.

RICHARD J. MEDALIE, LEONARD ZEITZ,
AND PAUL ALEXANDER

Custodial Police Interrogation in Our Nation's Capital: The Attempt To Implement Miranda

The Miranda Premises

In *Miranda,* the Court's aim was to devise proper safeguards which would preclude custodial police interrogation practices designed to impair a defendant's capacity to remain silent. Once a suspect in custody was to be questioned by police, he would have to be "adequately and effectively apprised of his rights" and assured of "a continuous opportunity to exercise them." To this end, the police were to warn the suspect "in clear and unequivocal terms"

—that he had the right to remain silent;
—that anything said "can and will" be used against the individual in court;
—that he had not only the right to consult with counsel prior to questioning, but also the right to have counsel present at the interrogation;
—that if he could not afford an attorney, one would be appointed for him prior to any questioning if the defendant so desired.

At least three related premises seemed to underlie the Court's decision: (1) that the police will give adequate and effective warnings of legal rights and will honor the accused's exercise of those rights; (2) that the defendant will understand the meaning of the warnings and their significance in application to himself and that he

From the *Michigan Law Review,* 66, no. 7 (May 1968), pp. 1347–1422. Reprinted by permission of the publisher and the authors.

Richard D. Medalie is the Director of the Institute of Criminal Law and Procedure at the Georgetown Law Center, Washington, D.C.

will thereby have sufficient basis to decide in his own best interest whether or not to remain silent and whether or not to request counsel; and (3) that the presence of an attorney in the police station will protect the accused's fifth amendment privilege.

The Nature of the Present Study

In order to test these premises, the Institute of Criminal Law and Procedure of the Georgetown University Law Center [1] undertook an empirical study of the attempt to implement *Miranda* in the District of Columbia.[2] In contrast to other studies which have concentrated on the police and law enforcement,[3] the Institute concerned itself

1. The Institute of Criminal Law and Procedure was established in October 1965 under a grant from the Ford Foundation, at the Georgetown University Law Center. The staff of the Institute is composed of attorneys and research associates from other disciplines, including sociology, psychiatry, psychology, social work, forensic science, history, and political science. The primary aim of the Institute is to engage in systematic studies of the criminal law process from police investigation practices to appellate and post-conviction procedures. The research for this article was conducted in a project of the Institute of Criminal Law and Procedure, under a grant from the Ford Foundation. The authors are greatly indebted to Samuel Dash, Director of the Institute, who provided helpful guidance and direction to the research throughout the course of the project and who contributed many useful suggestions during the writing of this article.

2. See Dash, *Foreword*, in R. MEDALIE, FROM ESCOBEDO TO MIRANDA: THE ANATOMY OF A SUPREME COURT DECISION xix (1966).

3. These studies analyzed police interrogation procedures in the following cities: (1) Boston, Chicago and Washington, D.C.: Reiss & Black, *Interrogation and the Criminal Process*, ANNALS OF THE AM. ACAD. OF POL. & SOC. SCI., Nov. 1967, at 47; see also Black & Reiss, *Patterns of Behavior in Police and Citizen Transactions*, in 2 PRESIDENT'S COMMISSION ON LAW ENFORCE-MENT AND ADMINISTRATION OF JUSTICE FIELD SURVEY III—STUDIES IN CRIME AND LAW ENFORCEMENT IN MAJOR METROPOLITAN AREAS 1 (Reiss ed. 1967). (2) Detroit: V. Piersante, Confession in Felony Prosecutions for the Year of 1961 as Compared to Jan. 20, 1965, through Dec. 31, 1965 (unpublished manuscript, July 27, 1965); see N.Y. Times, Feb. 28, 1966, at 18, col. 1. (3) Los Angeles: E. Younger, Results of Survey Conducted in the District Attorney's Office of Los Angeles County Regarding the Effects of the *Dorado* and *Miranda* Decisions upon the Prosecution of Felony Cases, Aug. 4, 1966. See also Younger, *Interrogation of Criminal Defendants—Some Views on Miranda v. Arizona*, 35 FORDHAM L. REV. 255 (1966). (4) New Haven: *Interrogation in New Haven: The Impact of Miranda*, 76 YALE L.J. 1519 (1967). See also Griffiths & Ayres, A Postscript to the Miranda Project: Inter-

primarily with the effect of *Miranda* on the role played by defense counsel at the stationhouse and on the defendant's perception of his legal rights. Moreover, unlike other studies which obtained data by stationing observers with the police,[4] the Institute obtained its data primarily through questionnaires administered to attorneys who had volunteered their time to service defendants at the stationhouse in a year-long "Precinct Representation Project," and through interviews with defendants in the Institute's Defendant Interview Study. To the extent permitted by the available data obtained from the attorneys and defendants, police warning and interrogation practices were also analyzed.

The Defendant Interview Study

To assess the impact of *Miranda* on the defendant directly, the Institute devised its Defendant Interview Study. The Institute staff conducted interviews with 260 persons who had been subjected to arrest procedures in the District of Columbia during 1965 and 1966.

The interview schedule was designed to gather a wide variety of data concerning (1) the defendant's reaction to actual and hypothetical arrest situations; (2) his attitudes toward the adversary system, the assistance of counsel, and police investigative practices; (3) his perception of constitutional and other legal rights coincident to arrest and initial presentment; (4) his awareness of judicial decisions defining those rights; and (5) his knowledge and understanding of the criminal law process itself.

---

rogation of Draft Protestors, 77 YALE L.J. 300 (1967). (5) New York: Sobel, *The Exclusionary Rules in the Law of Confessions: A Legal Perspective—A Practical Perspective,* 154 N.Y.L.J. 1 (1965). *See also* N. SOBEL, THE NEW CONFESSION STANDARDS 136–39 (1966). (6) Pittsburgh: Seeburger & Wettick, *Miranda in* PITTSBURGH—A STATISTICAL STUDY, 29 U. PITT. L. REV. 1 (1967).

4. *See, e.g.,* Reiss & Black, *supra* note 3, at 51–52; *Interrogation in New Haven, supra* note 3, at 1527–28, 1637–38. Although we attempted to conduct a similar observation study of the police in the District of Columbia, we were unable to work out satisfactory arrangements with the Metropolitan Police Department.

The Central Findings

Two central findings stand out in our study. First, approximately 40 per cent of the defendants in our study who were arrested in the post-*Miranda* period stated that they had given statements [5] to the police.[6] Second, an astonishingly small number of defendants—1,262 —requested counsel from the Precinct Representation Project, even though volunteer attorneys were readily available around the clock, seven days a week.[7] This number represented only 7 per cent of the 15,430 persons arrested for felonies and serious misdemeanors in the District of Columbia during fiscal 1967.

These central findings bring into question the three basic premises of *Miranda*. To assess their significance, we shall . . . explore the reaction of the defendants to the *Miranda* warnings—their understanding of the warnings, their attitudes toward the warnings, and their reasons for deciding whether or not to obtain counsel and whether or not to cooperate with the police. . . ." [A long statement of methodology follows. —ed.]

THE DEFENDANTS' REACTION TO THE MIRANDA WARNINGS

The Court's Reasons for Requiring the Warnings

James Mill in his *Essay on Government* propounded the view that a proper knowledge of one's self-interest would lead one to act in

---

5. As in *Miranda*, the term "statements" includes for purposes of the present study "statements which are direct confessions . . . statements which amount to 'admissions' of part or all of an offense . . . inculpatory statements and statements alleged to be merely 'exculpatory.' " Miranda v. Arizona, 384 U.S. 436, 467–77 (1966). In addition, for the sake of completeness, unrelated and uncharacterized statements are included in the definition and will be noted, where relevant.

6. A slightly higher percentage of defendants in our study who were arrested before *Miranda* also gave statements to the police. . . .

7. After the first month of operation of the Project, Julian Dugas, then head of the NLSP found it "incredible" that his attorneys had received so few calls. As he observed, "[S]ince the free legal service was organized . . . only 78 defendants have taken advantage of it. It seems extraordinary—in fact, it seems incredible—in light of the number of serious offenses committed each day in Washington." Washington Post, July 20, 1966, at C-1, col. 1.

accordance with that interest.[8] According to Mill's son, John Stuart, so complete was his father's "reliance on the influence of reason over the minds of mankind . . . that he felt as if all would be gained if the whole population were taught to read." [9] James Mill's "fundamental doctrine," said his son, "was the . . . unlimited possibility of improving the moral and intellectual condition of mankind by education." [10]

The underlying philosophy of the Court's decision in *Miranda* is closely akin to Mill's eighteenth century Utilitarian views. Implicit throughout the opinion is the assumption that once the defendant is properly warned of his legal rights he will be in a position to act in accordance with his interest in remaining silent and requesting a lawyer.

The Court's philosophical position may be most clearly seen in its characterization of the right-to-silence warning. The warning is needed, the Court avowed, in order to make the accused "aware" of the right.[11] In effect, the silence warning is "the threshold requirement for an intelligent decision as to its exercise." [12] It "insure[s] that the individual knows he is free to exercise the privilege at that point in time" [13] and shows the individual "that his interrogators are prepared to recognize his privilege should he choose to exercise it." [14] In like manner, the Court maintained, the warning that anything said can and will be used against the accused makes him aware "not only of the privilege but also of the consequences of foregoing it." [15] This awareness assures a "real understanding and intelligent exercise of the privilege" and serves to make the accused "more accurately aware that he is faced with a phase of the adversary system—that he

---

8. "[I]f the parties who act contrary to their interest had a proper knowledge of that interest, they would act well. What is necessary, then, is knowledge." J. Mill, *An Essay on Government*, in THE ENGLISH PHILOSOPHERS FROM BACON TO MILL 885 (1939).

9. J. MILL, AUTOBIOGRAPHY 89 (World Classics ed. 1931).

10. *Id.* at 91; *see also* J. PENNOCK, LIBERAL DEMOCRACY: ITS MERITS AND PROSPECTS 17 (1950).

11. 384 U.S. at 468.

12. 384 U.S. at 468.

13. 384 U.S. at 469.

14. 384 U.S. at 468.

15. 384 U.S. at 469.

is not in the presence of persons acting solely in his interest." [16]

Unfortunately, the Court's vision of how *Miranda* would operate has become somewhat blurred in practice, as our statistics of interrogation and confession demonstrate. We must therefore ask what did the *Miranda* warnings mean to the defendants and to what extent were they helped by the recital of warnings.

The Defendant's Behavior Following the Warnings

A definite relationship existed between the giving of the warning of the right to stationhouse counsel [17] and the "post-*Miranda* defendants'" decision to obtain counsel: close to two-thirds of these defendants who reported receiving this warning did request counsel. Yet the fact remains that over one-third of these defendants receiving the warning did not request counsel. Moreover, when no warnings were given or when warnings other than the right to stationhouse counsel were given, the overwhelming response of well over three-quarters of the remaining "post-*Miranda* defendants" was not to request counsel. The results are set forth in Table 1.

16. 384 U.S. at 469. The Court continued in this vein for the other warnings as well. Thus, concerning the right to the presence of an attorney, it said: "Only through such warning is there ascertainable assurance that the accused was aware of this right." 384 U.S. at 472. Concerning the right to an appointed counsel, the Court added:

> Without this additional warning, the admonition of the right to consult with counsel would often be understood as meaning only that he can consult with a lawyer if he has one or has the funds to obtain one. The warning of a right to counsel would be hollow if not couched in terms that would convey to the indigent—the person most often subjected to interrogation—the knowledge that he too has a right to have counsel present. As with the warnings of the right to remain silent and the general right to counsel, only by effective and express explanation to the indigent of this right can there be assurance that he was truly in a position to exercise it. [U.S. at 473]

17. The warnings we used were as follows:

> You have been placed under arrest. You are not required to say anything to us at any time or to answer any questions. Anything you say may be used against you as evidence in Court.
> Your lawyer may be present here during the police interrogation and you may consult with him.
> If you cannot afford to retain a lawyer privately, you have the right to have a lawyer appointed to represent you free of charge at the police station.

Table 1

RESULTS OF SPECIFIC WARNINGS OF POST-MIRANDA DEFENDANTS [a]

BY WHETHER COUNSEL REQUESTED [b]

Warnings of Rights	Counsel Requested		Counsel Not Requested	
	No.	%	No.	%
Non-stationhouse Counsel	2	17	10	83
Stationhouse Counsel	21	64	12	36
Silence Alone	3	23	10	77
Neither Counsel nor Silence [c]	3	12	21	88
Undetermined			3	* [d]
Total	29		56	

[a] Only 2 of the 175 pre-*Miranda* defendants requested counsel.
[b] Data source: Defendant Interview Schedules.
[c] Includes warnings of phone and/or bond, as well as no warning.
[d] Irrelevant or insignificant percentage.

Similarly, a parallel relationship existed between the warning of the right to silence and the "post-*Miranda* defendants'" refusal to give statements to the police: 60 per cent of these defendants who said they were given the warning gave no statements; the other 40 per cent, however, did give statements despite the warning. At the same time, when no silence or other warnings were said to have been given, over half of the remaining "post-*Miranda* defendants" gave statements to the police. . . .

The Defendant's Understanding of the Warnings

In order to test their cognitive understanding, we gave full *Miranda*-type warnings one at a time to the defendants, and, after each, asked what the warning meant to them.[18] The defendants' answers

18. Our interviewers gave these warnings to the defendants interviewed in as neutral a manner as possible. To be sure, this procedure could not duplicate the atmosphere at arrest or at the stationhouse, where the possible anxiety of the defendant and the possible partisan manner of the police (*see Interrogation in New Haven*, at 1552) would probably lead to greater misunderstanding and confusion as to the meaning of the warnings than was registered by the defendants in our interviews. Consequently, if anything, our results understate the defendants' rate of misunderstanding of the warnings.

were then rated as signifying either "understanding" or "misunderstanding." [19] The ratings indicated that 15 per cent of the eighty-five "post-*Miranda* defendants" failed to understand the right to silence warning, 18 per cent failed to understand the warning of the right to the presence of counsel, and 24 per cent failed to understand the warning of the right to appointed counsel.

We were able to derive an added insight into the defendants' understanding of the warnings by obtaining their verbatim comments of what they felt about the way the police told them of their rights. A number were cynical about the procedure, and believed the warnings to be "merely a formality" given to them only because the police "had to." Thus, one defendant complained that the police "didn't seem to care whether we understood or not," and another noted that the police officer giving the warnings "was as ignorant of my rights as I was myself. He was only reading a statement."

On the other hand, several other defendants accepted the warnings from the police at their face value. As one remarked, "They were helpful. [The police] . . . explained . . . [the warnings] very clearly, which is more than they used to do." Others remarked that "[t]hey talked like they meant it"; "they made a big thing about it"; "they wanted it to be known they had about eight people watching as witnesses."

There were many misconceptions as to the meaning of the right to stationhouse counsel. The following were typical misinterpretations of the warning by the defendants:

—The police "had some lawyer of their own who was working with them."

—It means that "I would have to pay for a lawyer."

—They planned to "appoint someone at court."

19. "Understanding" included both complete and partial understanding. Complete understanding was indicated either by an explanation which signified understanding or a definitional statement as to the specified right. A number of respondents answered by saying that the right "means just what it says." This response was considered to be a partial understanding. Our interviewers reported that the somewhat more educated or aggressive persons gave this response and resented any attempt at clarification. "Misunderstanding" included both complete and partial misunderstanding. Complete misunderstanding included the response, "I don't know." Partial misunderstanding included such responses as "That would mean I'm in trouble"; "That wouldn't mean anything to me since I'm innocent"; or "That would mean a lot to me."

—"I just have to write for one and wait for him to answer."

—"I don't know why one would need a lawyer in a stationhouse; it's never done."

—The warning "means I would answer [questions by the police] if a lawyer is present."

Other defendants were not even able to get to the point of interpreting the warning. For example, one was shown the police card with the warnings on it, but failed to read it, and another was so wrought up that his "mind wasn't functioning." "I couldn't think," he reported.

Some defendants had comparable misconceptions about the right to silence warning. Several understood it to mean that they had the right to talk. Some had the opposite impression that the police either did not want them to talk or would not let them talk. Others perceived a garbled version. As one said, it means that "I should have the right to say something so they can use it in evidence in court," and another added that it meant that "[I]f I . . . like try to bribe them, they would use it against me in court." Still others propounded more involved interpretations. "If I'm innocent," said one, "I should tell the truth." Another recognized the dilemma presented: [t]he warning means "that if I said anything false it would go hard on me; if I tell the truth, then trouble."

The Relationship of the Defendant's Understanding to His Behavior

More significant than the defendant's understanding of the warnings is the relationship of this understanding (or misunderstanding) to the decisions each defendant made concerning the right to counsel and the right to silence. . . . 66 per cent of those who understood the stationhouse counsel warning given by the police requested counsel, and approximately sixty per cent of those who understood the silence warning did not give statements.

The Inverse Relationship of Defendant's Understanding to His Behavior

A . . . question raised . . . is why the 34 per cent of the "post-*Miranda* defendants" who understood the counsel warnings did not request counsel and why the 41 per cent who understood the silence warning did not remain silent.

Several commentators have attempted explanation. Elsen and Rosett have observed:

> To predict how a suspect's insistence on his rights will affect his chances of avoiding prosecution requires an intimate knowledge of the system which cannot be conveyed by a warning, however improved. . . . The suspect . . . does not know if his request for counsel will annoy the police, the prosecutor or a jury. The fact that he has been warned as required by *Miranda* may have little bearing on his decision whether counsel should be waived. . . . A suspect may well choose not to be a "wise guy" who will land in jail as a reward for his insistence on his rights.[20]

And Wald and his fellow editors of the *Yale Law Journal* have noted:

> The suspect arrested and brought downtown for questioning is in a crisis-laden situation. The stakes for him are high—often his freedom for a few or many years—and his prospects hinge on decisions that must be quickly made: To cooperate and hope for leniency, to try and talk his way out, to stand adamantly on his rights . . . The likely consequences of the alternatives open to him are unclear —how much leniency cooperation may earn, how likely fast talk is to succeed, how much a steadfast refusal to talk may contribute to a decision by the police, prosecutor or judge to "throw the book" at him.[21]

Thus, while these defendants may have had a cognitive understanding of their rights, they had no appreciation of them and lacked the ability to apply them to their "crisis-laden" situations. This is borne out by many of the statements of the defendants we obtained in our interviews. Although these statements could not be quantitatively analyzed, they did afford us an opportunity to gain an insight into the reasons for rejection of counsel and for talking to the police.

Concerning the right to stationhouse counsel, one defendant did not believe he could really obtain a lawyer at the station. Another did not trust a lawyer furnished by the police. "I don't dig those jail-

20. Elsen & Rosett. *Protections for the Suspect under Miranda* 67 COLUM. L. REV. 645, 658 (1967).
21. *Interrogation in New Haven, supra,* at 1613–14.

house deals," he said. "The police have their own lawyer. I wouldn't be interested." And another added, "I only wanted to talk to people I could trust who would let me know what I was up against." Other defendants were too preoccupied with other concerns to recognize the value of a lawyer. Thus, one noted, "I wasn't thinking about anything but calling my mother and wife," and another's "main concern was bond." Still others believed that they themselves knew the system too well to risk having a lawyer. As one "sophisticated" defendant observed, "I wouldn't want one. That's the *worst* place to have a lawyer because the police play it straight then. I wanted them to make a mistake."

As for the right to silence, some feared being hit or beaten up by the police. Several maintained they had been threatened by the police or tricked. Another answered questions only because they did not relate to the charge against him. Still others wanted to convince police of their innocence. In this regard, a general response was that "I saw no harm in it," or that "I had nothing to hide," or that "I thought I was not at fault so I talked." One defendant insisted that there is always a tendency for a person to want to cooperate. And others explained that they would get lenient treatment if they cooperated. As a defendant said, "I figured I could straighten out the whole thing right there." Finally, there were those who just felt compelled to talk. As one explained, "I did it. I knew why the police wanted me, and they had me cold."

*   *   *

In light of the foregoing data on police practices under *Miranda* and the defendants' response, even in an optimum system of precinct representation, with well-trained counsel at the police station available as soon as a defendant is brought in, the odds against even beginning to approach the model established by the Court in *Miranda* would have been exceedingly high.

THEODORE SOURIS

Stop and Frisk or Arrest and Search—
The Use and Misuse of Euphemisms

* * *

One might begin by noting that this certainly is not the first time that a particular police practice, when assailed as violative of constitutional guarantees, has been defended on the ground that it is indispensable to effective law enforcement. That argument was made in the *Escobedo* case,[1] the meaning of which, as I read it, is that a suspect in police custody, before he is questioned for the purpose of obtaining a confession from him, must be accorded the absolute right to remain silent and to consult with counsel.[2]

We have been told, without reference to any authority but only by reference to hypothetical criminal situations, that "The only course open to the police in the overwhelming majority of these cases [of robbery, rape and others of a similar nature] is to look for probable suspects and question them as to their possible guilt." [3] And we have

1. Escobedo v. Illinois, 378 U.S. 478 (1964).
2. See People v. Dorado, 42 Cal. Rptr. 169, 398 P.2d 361 (1965).
3. Inbau, *Law Enforcement, the Courts and Individual Civil Liberties* in Criminal Justice in our Time 134–35 (1965), at 100.

From *The Journal of Criminal Law, Criminology and Police Science,* 57: 3 (Sept. 1966), pp. 254–55. Copyright © 1966 by Northwestern University School of Law. Reprinted by permission of the publisher and the author.

Theodore Souris was an Associate Justice of the Supreme Court of the State of Michigan. Since writing this article, he has returned to his private law practice in Detroit.

been told that in *Escobedo* the reason the police refused to permit the defendant's lawyer to see him before they had finished questioning him and obtaining his confession was because "the standard advice lawyers give to their clients in such situations is 'Keep your mouth shut.' " [4] The whole tenor of the article from which these quotations are taken is that if persons in custody are told of their constitutional rights to remain silent and to consult an attorney, or, even worse, if they actually are permitted to talk to a devilish advocate, whole hordes of robbers and rapists will swarm through the land undetected.

. . . I should like to refer to the report compiled by Chief of Detectives Vincent W. Piersante of the Detroit Police Department. . . . Chief Piersante compiled statistics of confessions and their use by several specialized bureaus of the Detroit Police Department for the year 1961 and for a nine-month period in 1965, that period commencing upon the date when the department began effective notification of criminal suspects of their absolute right to remain silent and their right to legal counsel.[5] Officers involved in the cases were inter-

4. *Id.* at 107.
5. On January 20, 1965, the following letter was sent to all commanding officers in the criminal investigation division:

"In view of the recent United States Supreme Court decision in the Case of Escobedo vs Illinois, which reversed a conviction on a murder charge by declaring a confession inadmissible, and then proceeded to set some definite guidelines for prisoner interrogation, the following is submitted as a procedure which we will follow:

"When an investigation is no longer a general inquiry into an unsolved crime, but has begun to focus on a particular suspect and the suspect has been taken into police custody, he must be effectively warned of his absolute constitutional right to remain silent. In addition, he must be provided with an opportunity to consult with his lawyer if he so requests.

"The following statement will be made by interrogating officers to the suspect at the beginning of the questioning: 'I am Detective (the officer should state his name), and I wish to advise you that you have a constitutional right to refuse to make any statement. You do not have to answer any questions which are put to you, and anything you do say may be used against you in a Court of Law in the event of prosecution. You are further advised that you have a right to counsel.'

"This notification of constitutional rights will be noted in the remarks section of the interrogation sheet, or some other appropriate place. It is also suggested that the suspect be requested to sign this section of the interrogation sheet, as further proof of the fact that he was informed of his rights under the

viewed and the files were reviewed to determine in what percentage of the prosecutions confessions were essential.

In robberies, in 1961, confessions were obtained in 81.8% of the cases, and they were deemed essential in 26% of the cases; in 1965, confessions were obtained in 83% of the cases and deemed essential in 29%. In forcible rapes, in 1961, confessions were obtained in 24.3% of the cases, and in 1965, in 19% of the cases; none of the confessions was deemed essential, because it is the policy of the department not to issue warrants in such cases upon the basis of a confession without extrinsic evidentiary support. Lumping all categories of crime surveyed, we find that in 1961 confessions were obtained in 60.8% of the cases, and were deemed essential in 13.1% of the cases; in 1965, confessions were obtained in 58% of the cases, but were deemed essential in only 11.3% of the cases.

What, then, were the results of "stripping the police of essential investigative procedures" by requiring, in the spirit of *Escobedo,* that suspects be informed of their rights to remain silent and to counsel? At the very least, improved police efficiency, as evidenced by the fact that reliance upon confessions, as the basis for convictions, decreased. Moreover, except in one category, burglary, there was no significant decrease in the number of confessions obtained after the department began effectively to notify prisoners of their rights, and in that category the decrease in the number of confessions obtained was more than offset by a greater decrease in the number of cases in which confessions were deemed essential, this fact attributable, no doubt, to a rising level of efficiency and competency among the officers of the department.

*   *   *

Law. (A separate form to be signed by the suspect is being considered and may be issued in the near future.)

"Certain statements by suspects are still admissible without the prescribed notification of their constitutional rights. These include 'threshold' statements which take place at the time of arrest and while the suspect is being transported to the Station. Thus it is imperative that arresting officers and officers at the scene of a crime make very specific and detailed reports of their actions and conversations with suspects prior to turning them over to Detectives for final investigation."

Appendix

DETROIT POLICE DEPARTMENT
CRIMINAL INVESTIGATION DIVISION

December 13, 1965

*Confessions in Felony Prosecutions for the Year of 1961 as
Compared to January 20, 1965, Through October 31, 1965*

* * *

HOMICIDE CASES

	1961	Percentage	1–20–65 to 10–31–65	Percentage
Prosecutions	115	—	107	—
Convictions	105	91.3	36	33.6
Pending	0	—	68	63.6
Confessions	61	53.0	60	56.1
Confessions Essential	24	20.9	10	9.3

NARCOTIC VIOLATIONS

	1961	Percentage	1–20–65 to 10–31–65	Percentage
Prosecutions	240	—	205	—
Convictions	197	82.1	69	33.7
Pending	3	1.3	119	59.0
Confessions	124	51.7	107	52.2

Confessions were not essential in any court case.

KIDNAPPING—EXTORTION—ARSON—LARCENY BY TRICK

	1961	Percentage	1–20–65 to 10–31–65	Percentage
Prosecutions	24	—	51	—
Convictions	9	37.5	25	49.0
Pending	0	—	24	47.1
Confessions	7	29.2	16	31.4
Confessions Essential	3	12.5	0	—

ROBBERIES

	1961	Percentage	1–20–65 to 10–31–65	Percentage
Prosecutions	181	—	112	—
Convictions	170	93.9	56	50.0
Pending	—	—	54	48.2
Confessions	148	81.8	83	74.1
Confessions Essential	47	26.0	29	25.9

BURGLARIES

	1961	Percentage	1–20–65 to 10–31–65	Percentage
Prosecutions	62	—	37	—
Convictions	60	96.8	27	73.0
Pending	0	—	8	21.6
Confessions	40	64.5	12	32.4
Confessions Essential	33	53.2	9	24.3

FORCIBLE RAPE

	1961	Percentage	1–20–65 to 10–31–65	Percentage
Prosecutions	74	—	63	—
Convictions	56	75.7	29	46.0
Pending	—	—	25	39.6
Confessions	18	24.3	12	19.0
Confessions Essential	0	—	0	—

It is the policy of the Wayne County Prosecutor's Office not to issue a warrant on confession alone.

GRAND TOTAL

	1961	Percentage	1–20–65 to 10–31–65	Percentage
Prosecutions	1445	—	1358	—
Convictions	1216	84.2	768	56.6
Pending	3	.2	519	38.2
Confessions	879	60.8	787	58.0
Confessions Essential	189	13.1	153	11.3

The above figures are felony prosecutions handled by the Specialized Bureaus of the Criminal Investigation Division during the periods specified.

VINCENT W. PIERSANTE
Chief of Detectives

21 States Pressing for Reapportionment Amendment

Twenty-one of the required 34 state legislatures (two-thirds of the 50) have petitioned Congress to call a constitutional convention to write an amendment limiting the Supreme Court's authority over state legislative apportionment, a Congressional Quarterly survey shows. The state legislature action constitutes a significant pressure on Congress to act on its own to write and submit an amendment which would modify the Supreme Court's "one man, one vote" decisions. Hearings on a constitutional amendment were held in 1964 by the House Judiciary Committee and began again March 3 before the Senate Judiciary Constitutional Amendments Subcommittee.

BACKGROUND

Proposals for limiting the power of the courts in the reapportionment field have been prevalent since the Supreme Court, in its landmark March 1962 decision in *Baker v. Carr,* the Tennessee apportionment case, ruled that issues of constitutionality in apportionment matters were justiciable.

The General Assembly of the States (part of the Council of State Governments) in 1962 proposed a resolution completely removing federal court jurisdiction in apportionment matters. Sixteen of the states subsequently passed resolutions asking Congress to call a constitutional convention to write such an amendment:

Arkansas	Nebraska	Utah
Idaho	Nevada	Virginia
Kansas	Oklahoma	Washington
Mississippi	South Carolina	Wyoming
Missouri	South Dakota	
Montana	Texas	

From the *Congressional Quarterly*, 23 (March 5, 1965), pp. 339–40. Reprinted by permission of the publisher.

Then, in June 1964, the Supreme Court handed down additional reapportionment decisions, substantially widening the scope of the *Baker* decision. The new Court orders specified that both houses of state legislatures must be apportioned on a population basis (invalidating the so-called "little federal plan"). The Court also said that population must be substituted even if the voters of the state (as in Colorado and others) had specifically approved a non-population base for one body of their state legislature. (1964 Weekly Report p. 1218)

The new decisions significantly increased the pressure for some type of amendment to limit the Court's powers in the apportionment field. Stopgap efforts to bar court-ordered reapportionment were proposed in Congress in 1964 but were blocked by a determined filibuster by Senate liberals. (1964 Weekly Report p. 2384)

Opponents of the Court's position then turned to the regular constitutional amendment route, hoping for affirmative action in 1964. The General Assembly of the States, meeting Dec. 3, 1964, approved a resolution calling for an amendment which would permit one house of a bicameral state legislature to apportion on geography or some other non-population base, providing the arrangement was approved by the people of the state in a referendum. This new amendment, significantly milder than the one recommended in 1962, was similar to one backed by Senate Minority Leader Everett McKinley Dirksen (R Ill.) and introduced again in the 89th Congress (S J Res 2). Backers of the same or similar amendments included Rep. William M. McCulloch (R Ohio), his party's ranking member on the House Judiciary Committee, and Sen. Jacob K. Javits (R N.Y.). It was endorsed Feb. 8 by the American Bar Assn. (Weekly Report p. 246)

As of March 2, 17 states were on record as calling for a constitutional convention to write a constitutional amendment on this newer, more moderate pattern:

Alabama	Missouri
Arizona	Montana
Arkansas	New Mexico
Georgia	Nevada
Idaho	Oklahoma
Kansas	South Carolina

South Dakota   Texas
Tennessee   Utah
                                Virginia

The action of these states brought to 21 the total of states which, since 1962, had petitioned for a constitutional convention to write some type of new amendment on the apportionment problem.

In addition, the Senates of Alaska, California, Colorado, Maryland, North Dakota, Oregon and Wyoming, and the House in Vermont, had asked for a constitutional amendment on the newer, moderate pattern. The California Assembly memorialized Congress to submit an amendment along this line.

CURRENT OUTLOOK

The flurry of requests by the states for a constitutional convention, all directed toward limiting the scope of the Supreme Court's "one man, one vote" decisions, serves to counteract the basic political tide running in favor of the Supreme Court's decisions. Before the states took this action, the outlook for a constitutional amendment was fairly dark. The widespread victories of liberal Democrats in the 1964 elections—mostly candidates with their power bases in the cities or suburbs—promised to intensify the strong support for "one man, one vote" which had evidenced itself during the 1964 Senate filibuster. At least, the increase in liberal Democratic strength made it more difficult to win backing of two-thirds of both houses for a restrictive amendment.

But if opponents of the Court decisions are able to get two-thirds of the states to call for a constitutional convention, the chance for some type of action may increase dramatically. Once the requisite number of states (34) were to take this action, it would only require a majority vote in each house of Congress to actually convene a constitutional convention—not the two-thirds vote required if Congress writes an amendment and submits it directly to the states for ratification. If backers of some type of restrictive amendment clearly had majority backing in Congress, the liberals who oppose any modification of "one man, one vote" might decide to permit submission of a relatively mild constitutional amendment rather than risk the calling of a constitutional convention—which would, under the Constitution, actually be free to write any kind of amendment on any subject it chose.

A possible stumbling block for the backers of a constitutional amendment would be the determination of what actually constitutes a proper request by two-thirds of the states for calling of a constitutional convention. If absolutely identical resolutions were adopted by the states, Congress would clearly be under moral and political pressure to call the convention. But what if—as in the case of the apportionment resolutions—the resolutions varied in wording and as to the specifics of the amendment proposed? There are no precedents on this point, since the constitutional convention route has not been employed in the preparation of any of the 24 amendments to the Constitution. But constitutional scholars believe that the moral and political pressure on Congress to act, even if the exact wording of the state resolutions varied somewhat, might prove near irresistible. (The wording of Article V, on amendments, suggests that absolutely precise requests from the states are not required.) As for the possibility that the courts might be asked to block a constitutional convention called on the basis of slightly differing state resolutions, a 1939 Supreme Court decision (*Coleman v. Miller*) appears to establish the principle that the amending process is an exclusively political one in which the courts will not interfere.

On balance, however, most observers still feel that the possibility of a constitutional convention is merely being used as a bargaining tool to persuade Congress to write and submit an apportionment amendment directly to the states for ratification. Unless that move succeeds fairly soon, however, so many of the states may be apportioned on a pure population base that the amendment would be rejected by the states.

MARTIN LANDAU

Baker v. Carr *and the Ghost of Federalism*

* * *

American society is all the time "becoming." But the pace of change
—national and international, technological and social, technical and
scientific—is so swift that newly generated needs threaten our ability
to design new coping instruments. Even more important, however,
old instruments, once functional but now quite obstructive, possess
a capacity for resistance that challenge a necessary freedom to adapt.
Nowhere is this more clearly in evidence than in the election process
itself. The logic of our system requires that politics center itself
nationally, but the lack of a national party system is the most con-
spicuous anachronism of our time.

This "lag" which political scientists, almost as a group, attribute to
federalism was especially noted by the Committee on Political Parties
of the American Political Science Association. "The American political party," it stated, "has its roots in the states. Its regulation and
control is conducted almost wholly, although not entirely, by the
states acting separately." The consequence of this is clear: "The party
system is weighted much more heavily toward the state-local side
than is true today of the federal system of government in the United
States. *The gap produces serious disabilities in government. It needs
to be closed.*" [1]

1. "Toward a More Responsible Two-Party System," *Report of the Committee
on Political Parties,* American Political Science Association (1950), p. 26.
Emphasis added. See also David Truman, "Federalism and the Party System"
in Arthur Macmahon, *Federalism Mature and Emergent* (1955).

From *Reapportionment* by Glendon Schubert. Copyright © 1965 by Charles
Scribner's Sons. Reprinted by permission of the publisher and the author.

Martin Landau is Professor of Political Science at Brooklyn College of the
City University of New York.

185

This, in my judgment, is the historic function of *Baker* v. *Carr*: to close this gap. Tendencies in this direction—in the direction of national parties—have long been observed. It would be a curiosity indeed if the party system remained immune to the press of society. For these tendencies to become characteristic features of our political life, however, requires that the constitutional authorizations of another day be laid aside. It is precisely because the Constitution has traditionally secured such powers as apportionment to the states that a fractionized and decentralized party system has been maintained. The historic justification of this has been the value of local representation but the systems of apportionment in practice have sustained only a spurious and, at best, a technical local interest. The rural areas came first, assumed control and yielded, if at all, only very slowly to the urban shift which, most significantly lies at the base of a national politics.

Justice Harlan's dissent sets the sole issue of *Baker* v. *Carr* as "the right of a state to fix the basis of representation in its own legislature." [2] The Court's decision, he adds, means "to turn our backs on the regard which . . . has always been shown for the judgment of state legislatures and courts *on matters of basically local concern*." [3]

And this is the point. The decision in *Baker* v. *Carr* is quite to the contrary: The basis of representation for a state legislature is no longer a matter of basic local concern. The Court decision may be interpreted as a move to sustain the urban-national requirements of our time. Justice Frankfurter remarks on the battle between forces whose influence is disparate among the various organs of government. "No shift of power but works a corresponding shift in political influence among the groups composing a society." [4] By the nature of the issue involved, the effect of this decision will be to decrease the power and influence of rural interests and increase the power of metropolitan-urban areas. This will lessen the distance between urban centers and state governments. It will minimize certain types of conflict, allow for more effective planning, and enable a more coordinate attack on pressing urban problems.

The urbanization of state legislatures will be a relatively slow

2. 369 U.S. 331.
3. *Ibid.*, 332. Emphasis added.
4. *Ibid.*, 299.

process. It will involve much litigation and conflict. It will involve the courts directly; it will lead to efforts to revamp state constitutions; it will be fought out in the polls as the prime political issue it promises to become. And it will be accompanied by the urbanization of state politics.

The ultimate effect of this shift will be to weight the party system toward the urban-national side as against the state-local side and this is a necessary condition for the emergence of a national party system. To augment an already developing bypass of the state via direct national-metropolitan relationships with a national party system that is built upon an urban basis must mean a fundamental restructuring of our formal system of government. *Baker* v. *Carr* is a decision on the functional merits of federalism; it does strike deep into its heart.

Is this such a "massive repudiation of our past"? Or is it a development on our past? Once upon a time this country embarked on a voyage to nationhood. The journey was started by the institution of federalism. Its success in enabling a nation to evolve must by the nature of the instrument signal its own demise. The more we become an integrated nation, the less the need for federalism. It is one of those instruments so designed as to outmode itself by its achievements. Sixty years ago New York City was formed as a federal union. The object was to build a unified and coordinate city. This achievement rendered the boroughs quite impractical sixty years later. The life of this city is also marked by a steady transfer of authority to the central government to the point that borough governments exist now in name only. The recent charter proposals remove the last area of governmental activity from these "states." Within the context of evolution "whatever is useful must in the nature of life become useless." Federalism in this country has been a dramatic success.

4 Impact on Public Opinion

John Kessel stated in 1966 that it "is clear that we need a good national study of attitudes about the Court as soon as possible." He had just completed a research project on attitudes toward the Supreme Court on the part of a small sample of people living in the Seattle area, the results of which cried for replication on a much larger scale. Almost simultaneously, though, Professors Walter Murphy and Joseph Tanenhaus received funding from the National Science Foundation to conduct a coast-to-coast survey much along these lines. Subsequently, in the Fall of 1967, several preliminary findings of the Murphy-Tanenhause survey were reported at the Shambaugh Conference of Judicial Research held at the University of Iowa.[1] Also, another major study on attitudes toward the Supreme Court, this one by Kenneth Dolbeare, appeared in mid-1967.[2] It consisted of a detailed analysis of parts of (1) Gallup Polls dating back to 1937; (2) the Survey Research Center's (University of Michigan) national post-1964 election poll; and (3) a Wisconsin-wide survey supervised by the Wisconsin Survey Research Laboratory. A whole new area of empirical research in political science was opening, and opening fast.

1. See "Public Opinion and the United States Supreme Court," Joel Grossman and Joseph Tanenhaus (eds.), *New Frontiers in Judicial Research* (N.Y.: Wiley, 1969).
2. Kenneth Dolbeare, "The Public Views the Supreme Court," in Herbert Jacob (ed.), *Law, Politics and the Federal Courts* (Boston: Little, Brown, 1967).

Some readers may wonder what all the fuss is about. These skeptics only need to be reminded that public attitudes toward specific Court decisions have much to do with Congressional reactions and with degrees and types of local compliance. Therefore stockpiling data on public opinion about the Court *now* so as to understand (and possibly forecast) future responses to a Supreme Court decision would be an end sufficient unto itself, but there is another worthwhile reason as well.

Political science wants to see the effect of particular Court decisions on the more general popular attitudes toward the Supreme Court as a governmental institution and toward its general role and performance. What is so important about this? One major responsibility of modern political theory is to test the veracity of all significant aspects of political theory no matter how much wisdom they appear to contain. Modern political scientists are alert to the fact that much ideology lurks about posing as empirical (objective) political theory. In other words, to sway others to accept a particular political position, men have been known to couch a simple value preference ("I like") in the guise of a tested theory ("It is true that . . ."). Indeed, a good deal of the "theory" about the *functions* of the Supreme Court appear to be more ideology than verified theory. As it develops, a science of politics would become more and more capable of exposing ideology as it relates to how the Court is functioning.

For example, one of the hoariest and most salient propositions on the functions of the Supreme Court involves "legitimacy." According to Charles Black, Yale law professor and celebrated Court apologist, the mere power of judicial review, as brandished by the Court, confers a stamp of legitimacy upon *all* official acts of government, thereby lending a general air of legitimacy throughout American society.[3] In other words, Black argues that the bald possibility that *any* law can be declared unconstitutional by the Court affords an "air" of legality to *all* acts of American government (that is the envy of people everywhere).[4] His argument is well-reasoned at a high

3. Charles Black, *The People and the Court* (N.Y.: Macmillan, 1960), pp. 34 *et seq.*
4. Black believes this "air" possesses a "sweetness" to which Frenchmen are peculiarly unaccustomed. *Ibid.*, p. 35.

level of abstraction, but on closer inspection there is a certain lack of clarity and a distinct paucity of fact. For one thing, what is legitimacy and an air of legality anyway? Next, what conditions in brute reality indicate its existence? What conditions support it at low or high levels? To paraphrase Gertrude Stein's last, last words, modern political science has begun to ask, "What are the questions?" and to expect some exactitude in the asking of them. It is only because political science has matured so that some relevant facts have begun to emerge.

For instance, in order for the Court (acting as an institution) to legitimate anything, its decisions must have visibility. Legitimacy, after all is said and done, must imply a certain level of recognition in the society of specific actions taken by the Court as well as some knowledge about the general power of judicial review. The two studies in this section treat the level of public knowledge about the Court's case work; that is, about its specific decisions or about types of decisions the Court has made. But once the general problem of visibility has been raised, other more detailed questions arise too. What is the exact or approximate size of the community that must be aware of the Court's actions, or what particular segments of the community must have this awareness? The educated? The leaders? Over fifty per cent of the mass? How detailed should their knowledge be about the Court's decisions? How favorably must they view this work? Besides this, in order for there to be legitimacy there must be a certain type or level of public support for the role of judicial review and favorable opinion to the effect that the Court is performing judicial review properly. Again, who or how many must know and approve?

Generally, political scientists are garnering data and analyzing the connection of various factors (such as political culture, the political party identification of respondents, their degree of political alienation, their age, the region of the country in which they live) with their views on (a) specific Court decisions, (b) lines of cases decided by the Court, and (c) the institutional role and function of the Court. The following essays by Kessel and Dolbeare are excellent representatives of some aspects of this major, new line of inquiry.

Mr. Dooley once observed that the Supreme Court watched the election returns. As political science research on popular attitudes toward the Court evolves, the justices may begin to find the results equally worth watching. On second thought, they might find it worthwhile even in its present-day, early stages.

JOHN H. KESSEL

Public Perceptions of the Supreme Court

. . . This paper reports an exploratory study of attitudes about the United States Supreme Court. . . .

*   *   *

A two-stage probability sample was drawn from two state legislative districts, the 32nd and the 43rd, located within the city of Seattle. Taken together, the two districts included upper middle class, lower middle class, and working class residents. In addition, their location adjacent to the University of Washington offered the incidental advantage of easy access for the student interviewers. Four hundred and five interviews were actually completed.

The data reported in this paper are based on 356 of these interviews.

*   *   *

. . . It is clear that our Seattle sample varies from the national sample in important respects. The Seattle sample contains more political independents, more persons with college education, more members of the middle class, and more Caucasians. Hence this paper should be regarded simply as an analysis of the attitudes of persons we happened to interview. This analysis does contain a number of interesting suggestions about what the attitudes of a national popu-

From the *Midwest Journal of Political Science*, 10 (May 1966), pp. 167–91. Reprinted by permission of the Wayne State University Press.

John H. Kessel is Arthur E. Brown Professor of Political Science at Allegheny College.

lation might be. These should be read, however, as hypotheses in need of verification, rather than as generalizations which are warranted on the basis of our sample.

I

Just what are the public attitudes about the Court? These attitudes were measured in two ways. The first was an open-ended question (Speaking generally, how would you describe your own feelings about the Supreme Court?) and two associated probes, (Is there anything (else) you particularly like about the Supreme Court? Is there anything (else) you particularly dislike about the Supreme Court?). The answers to these questions were scaled by assigning a $+ 1$ to each positive comment and a $- 1$ to each negative comment, and then calculating a sum for each respondent.

The second means of ascertaining opinions about the Supreme Court was a series of questions about the preferred role of the Court (What do you think the job of the Supreme Court should be? Do you think the Supreme Court is doing this job now?). This sequence of questions was concluded with a standard query about intensity (How strongly do you hold these views? Very strongly? Fairly strongly? Or doesn't this make too much difference to you?). The intensity items were combined with the responses about whether the respondent thought the Court was doing its job to form a Likert scale. . . . However measured, the attitudes were supportive of the Court. . . .

*　　*　　*

The second largest category of supportive responses (9.9% of the respondents) stressed the need for a Supreme Court. Though unable to say why, these persons felt that we had to have one. A machinist put it this way:

> I'd say it has been with us . . . (pause) . . . since government started. It's a useful and necessary part of the government. That's what I'd say off hand.

A smaller group of respondents (4.8% of the total) made the point that the Court was doing its best with a difficult job. . . .

* * *

The largest number of critical answers were coded under the miscellaneous heading of "other critical comments." This category included 10.4% of the total. On examination, it appeared that many of these answers came from persons who disapproved of Supreme Court holdings. Although they were as well informed as most of the other people we interviewed, many of the persons in this category seemed disturbed about legal complexities they could not understand. An insurance adjuster described his feelings as:

> Generally unfavorable. The outcome as to what is constitutional or unconstitutional depends too much on one individual. The Court recently has been relying too much on technicalities to let the guilty off. One little error and they let a guy go free. In the area of criminal law, they seemed to be concerned with "Did Oswald get a free trial?"! Well, they had enough on him to kill him anyway—so why worry about detail?

* * *

Nine per cent of the respondents said that they felt the Supreme Court was acquiring too much power or that it was going beyond its proper role. . . .

Another group of critics, three per cent of the sample, felt that the Court was too favorable to some particular class. Sometimes this favored category of litigants was thought to be wealthy, sometimes not. . . .

Finally, a little more than a fifth of our sample (21.4%) was unable to articulate any opinion about the Supreme Court. Nearly two-thirds of these individuals stated frankly that they didn't feel they knew enough to have an opinion. A small businessman who had just bought a new sound truck company admitted:

> I've never given it much thought.

* * *

Similar characteristics were to be found in the responses to the queries about the preferred role of the Supreme Court. A typical answer to the question "What do you think the job of the Supreme Court should be?" was that of an elderly man:

> To study the law, I guess, and help decide what it should be for everyone.

Most of the answers to this question likewise revealed considerable attitudinal support for the Court resting upon a modest understanding of what the Court actually was about.

The distribution of the answers about the preferred role of the Supreme Court . . . is perhaps significant that taken together they add up to a composite portrait of the tasks which presently concern the Supreme Court. The Court is our tribunal of ultimate appeal. It does interpret the Constitution and the laws according to specified and impartial procedure. And so on. Since the Court is now doing what most of our respondents want it to do, it should follow that most of them will support it. This would suggest that how the Court reaches its decisions may be quite as important in maintaining public support as what it decides.

This is not to say that the content of the Supreme Court decisions is unimportant in shaping the public perception of that institution. While it is true that only a few cases are sufficiently dramatic to rise above the public's threshold of attention, these decisions do stimulate some public discussion. When our respondents were asked what they had read or heard about the Supreme Court during the last year, three-quarters of them referred to Court activity or decisions in four areas: civil rights, prayers in schools, redistricting, and Communists. Civil rights was mentioned by twice as many people as school prayers, school prayers by twice as many people as redistricting, and redistricting by twice as many people as referred to Communists. The exact percentages were civil rights, 42.0%; school prayers, 19.6%; redistricting, 8.0%; and Communism, 4.5%.

This was a bit of luck because the four areas most discussed happened to be the four subjects about which the respondents had been asked to decide "hypothetical" cases. The responses to these queries were related to attitude about the Court. A decision in favor of the public accommodations section, against a required school prayer, for "one man, one vote," and against sending a person to jail simply because he was a Communist was associated with a favorable view of the Supreme Court. The rank-order correlations (Kendall's Tau-b) between these hypothetical decisions and attitudes toward the Court were Heart of Atlanta Motel, .25, Schempp, .14, Wesberry v. Sanders, .12, and Scales, .18.

When the findings about the frequency of discussion of controversial topics are juxtaposed with the tendency to decide hypothetical cases in particular ways, it is possible to conclude something about how each of these decisions contributed to public attitudes about the Court. Civil rights activities are being widely discussed and the activities of the Court are well thought of in this area. The school prayer case and redistricting are being discussed by smaller groups of people and are having less effect on general attitudes about the Court. And while the Court's handling of Communists is being discussed by fewer people than any of the other three subjects, a person who mentions this topic is rather more likely to be critical of the Court.

II

Why do people hold these attitudes about the Supreme Court? What disposes some to have a favorable view of it while others have an unfavorable image? The answer to this simple question is rather complicated. In order to thread our way through the jumble of evidence, we shall confine our attention to a single dependent variable, the respondent's opinion of the Court as measured by the number of positive and negative comments about it, and use a single measure of association, Kendall's Tau-b.

If pure measures of attitudes could be devised, it might be possible to explain attitudes toward the Court on the basis of three independent variables: some measure of liberalism-conservatism, agreement with what the Court has done, and the favorability of communications received about the Court. Or, if one could tap basic attitudes about the cases before the Supreme Court, one might be able to construct an explanation using just these attitudes and what the respondent has read or heard about the Court's activities. This study, however, was not designed in any experimental utopia. We shall have to do the best we can with four independent variables: subjective party identification, support for specific free speech and procedural rights, agreement with four controversial decisions made by the Court, and the favorability of information received about the Court.

*   *   *

. . . Table 1 shows that favorability of prior information—as party identification, support for specific procedural rights, and agreement with Court decisions—did have an effect on attitudes about the Supreme Court.

*   *   *

. . . [H]aving pro-Court attitudes (being a Democrat, supporting 7 to 9 procedural rights, agreeing with 3 or 4 decisions) seems to explain much of what one hears and reads about the Court. At the same time, favorable information makes it less necessary to have such an attitude in order to take a pro-Court position. This implies a circular relationship in which the attitudes of the majority and the communications heard most frequently feed upon and support one another. The minority attitudes (being a Republican, agreeing with 2 or fewer Court decisions) are strong enough to survive in a hostile informational environment, but when persons holding these attitudes do encounter relatively rare anti-Court information, their attitudes are sharply reinforced.

There are several means of noting the joint influence of the four variables. One is to combine classes so that one group has several pro-Court influences. For example, one can create one group made up of Democrats who support 7 to 9 specific procedural rights and who agree with 3 or 4 Court decisions; a second made up of Independents who support 5 or 6 specific procedural rights and who agree with 2 Court decisions; and a third made up of Republicans who support no more than 4 specific procedural rights and who did not agree with more than 1 decision made by the Court. Such a classification of persons who should be pro-Court, neutral, and anti-Court, respectively, produces a Tau-b of .36 when checked against attitudes

Table 1

OPINIONS OF SUPREME COURT IN TERMS OF SELECTED VARIABLES ~

Independent Variable Party Identification	Attitude about the Supreme Court			
	Strong Supporter (+ 2 or higher)	Supporter (+ 1)	Neutral (0)	Critic (−1 or lower)
Strong Dem	28.4%	22.7%	10.5%	7.1%
Weak Dem	12.5	14.7	18.4	7.1
Independent Dem	20.5	14.7	18.4	13.1
Independent	11.4	13.3	10.5	10.7
Independent Rep	12.5	13.3	14.5	20.2
Weak Rep	10.2	12.0	13.2	15.5
Strong Rep	4.5	9.3	14.5	26.2
	100.0	100.0	100.0	100.0
N	88	75	76	84
Tau-b = .244				

Support for Specific Procedural Rights (McClosky Items)				
Support 7–9 Rights	56.2%	25.6%	26.2%	24.7%
Support 5 or 6 Rights	22.5	37.2	34.2	42.4
Support 0–4 Rights	21.3	37.2	39.5	32.9
	100.0	100.0	100.0	100.0
N	89	78	76	85
Tau-b = .163				

Agreement with Court Decisions				
Agree 3 or 4 Cases	46.0%	30.8%	26.9%	29.6%
Agree with 2 Cases	34.9	39.7	30.8	35.7
Agree 0 or 1 Case	19.5	29.5	42.3	35.7
	100.0	100.0	100.0	100.0
N	87	78	78	84
Tau-b = .144				

Prior Information				
Quite Favorable	35.1%	35.6%	20.0%	7.1%
Favorable	33.3	28.9	24.0	25.7
Mixed	15.8	24.4	20.0	30.0
Unfavorable	12.3	4.4	28.0	20.0
Quite Unfavorable	3.5	6.7	8.0	17.1
	100.0	100.0	100.0	100.0
N	57	45	25	70
Tau-b = .287				

about the Court. This is a higher degree of association than any one of the attitudinal variables produced by themselves.

The difficulty with this approach is that these four variables are somewhat independent of each other. If all Democrats agreed with the decisions of the Court, or if all Republicans were opposed to procedural and free speech rights, it would be easy to divide the world of Court perceptions into liberal and conservative and be done with it. But this is *not* the case. . . .

* * *

III

Who are the supporters of the Court? Who are its critics? Which persons are neutral in their opinions of the Court? The most direct answer is that every type of person is to be found in each category. These attitudes were analyzed in terms of a series of demographic variables: age, sex, education, religion, occupation, union membership, social class, income and ancestry. No significant relationships were found. As a general explanation for the existence of these attitudes, a demographic approach is not very powerful.

If, however, we are careful to keep in mind that we are working with weak statistical tendencies rather than with any cause and effect relationships, there are some things which can be noted. The most important findings are presented in Table 2. The effect of age is noticeable in that those under 30 are most inclined to be strong supporters of the Court, while those over 50 are likely to be critical. Men are more likely to be found among the strong supporters or critics of the Court, while women are much more likely to be neutral. Education appears to have a similar, if weaker, effect. Those with college degrees are found disproportionately among those who are strong supporters or critics while those who did not go beyond high school tend to be among those who are neutral or weak supporters.

* * *

To the extent that any generalizations can be drawn from these rather weak relationships, there is one theme which runs through

Table 2

OPINIONS OF SUPREME COURT IN TERMS OF SELECTED
DEMOGRAPHIC VARIABLES

Demographic Variable	Opinion of Supreme Court			
	Strong	Supporter	Neutral	Critic
Age *				
Under 30	33.3%	26.9%	29.1%	17.6%
30–49	36.6	34.6	30.3	37.6
Over 50	30.1	38.5	40.6	44.8
N	90	78	79	85

$$C = .25, X^2 = 21.806, .20 > p > .10$$

Sex				
Male	55.6%	50.0%	37.5%	55.3%
Female	44.4	50.0	62.5	44.7
N	90	78	80	85

$$C = .14, X^2 = 7.061, .10 > p > .05$$

Education				
Not H. S. Graduate	12.8%	19.4%	14.9%	16.0%
H. S. Graduate	26.7	30.6	31.1	18.5
Some College	24.4	27.8	28.4	24.7
College Graduate	36.0	22.2	25.7	40.7
N	86	72	74	81

$$C = .17, X^2 = 10.006, .40 > p > .30$$

* These data are presented in condensed form in the interests of clarity. The statistics for the data, however, were calculated on the basis of 6 age categories.

the data. This is that the supporters and critics of the Court have more in common with each other than either grouping does with those who take a neutral posture. This holds up when one looks at intensity of opinion. Strong supporters have the same demographic characteristics as strong opponents. Mild supporters resemble mild critics. And so on.

There are exceptions to this. It would be a fairly good bet that a young Jew or a young Italian-American would take a pro-Court position. But a middle-aged man with a college education whose ancestors came from England who had a white collar job and a moderately high income would be likely to have a strong attitude in one direction *or* the other. On the other hand, an older woman with little formal education whose ancestors came from Poland and whose late husband had been a laborer would be likely to lack any firm attitude or, at most, to take a neutral posture. As we read back over these characteristics, the meaning of the differences becomes more obvious. The socio-economic groups who take neutral stances are those who are more isolated from our political culture. Hence, *having an attitude depends on being involved in the political culture while the direction of the attitude depends on the nature of the political environment to which one is exposed.*

If questions can be raised about the weak demographic relationships in Table 2, they can be answered with additional data which support the same conclusions. In Table 3, attitudes about the Court are compared with some measures of involvement in the political culture. We first note that those who have talked about or read about the Supreme Court during the past year are more likely to be found among the supporters or critics of the Court than among those who are neutral. We also see that critics are more likely to have paid some attention to the Court than its supporters. The same thing is true regarding persons who gave some indication in the course of the interview that they were aware of at least one of the four controversial areas in which the Court had been active. A third measure of involvement, intensity of feeling about the Supreme Court, is related to the respondents' comments in a way we have come to expect. Supporters of the Court tend to hold their opinions fairly strongly, more opponents of the Court hold their opinions very strongly; and those who are neutral are also likely not to care too much one way or another. . . .

IV

Now let us recapitulate our major points. Important differences were found between those who had attitudes about the Supreme Court and those who did not. Essentially the differences between those who had attitudes and those who did not were the differences between the politically involved and the politically isolated. Among those possessing attitudes, the direction of the attitude concerning the Court was jointly determined by a cluster of related political attitudes and by

Table 3

OPINIONS OF SUPREME COURT IN TERMS OF POLITICAL INVOLVEMENT

Measure of Involvement	Opinion of Supreme Court			
Read or Heard about Court in Last Year?	Strong Supporter	Supporter	Neutral	Critic
Yes	73.3%	68.5%	45.2%	89.2%
No	26.7	31.5	54.8	10.8
N	86	76	73	83

$$C = .32, X^2 = 36.275, p < .001$$

Heard about Cases Before?				
Yes	70.1%	57.9%	48.7%	78.6%
No	29.9	42.1	51.3	21.4
N	87	76	76	84

$$C = .23, X^2 = 18.187, p < .001$$

Intensity of Attitude about Court				
Very Strong	40.9%	34.2%	17.5%	51.8%
Fairly Strong	48.9	39.7	39.7	32.5
Doesn't Care	10.2	26.0	42.9	15.7
N	88	73	63	83

$$C = .31, X^2 = 36.543, p < .001$$

Number of Political Activities				
5–6	10.1%	12.8%	3.9%	8.8%
1–4	73.0	61.6	68.8	71.8
0	16.9	25.6	27.3	14.1
N	89	78	77	85

$$C = .19, X^2 = 12.58, p = .05$$

communications concerning the Court. . . . Finally, the over-all distribution of attitudes was favorable to the Supreme Court.

There are important implications in these findings relating to the probability of changes in these attitudes. We have three types of respondents, each of which has rather different characteristics. Let us ask what would happen to each in the event that pro-Court or anti-Court propaganda were directed at them. Supporters of the Court are already receiving a sufficient number of pro-Court communications to maintain their attitudes. Additional pro-Court messages might result in a modest strengthening of their attitudes, but this is about all. Anti-Court communications, on the other hand, are unlikely to come to their attention at all because their attitudes produce such a high threshold of awareness. Identical threshold mechanisms make it unlikely that those who are now neutral in their stance would be aware of either pro-Court or anti-Court propaganda. In addition, their isolation from our political culture makes it improbable that they would have much contact with political communications to begin with. The critic of the Court is not likely to assimilate pro-Court propaganda, but an increase in the frequency with which he encounters anti-Court communications can perceptibly increase the intensity of his conviction. In sum, the minority may become more highly motivated but is unlikely to become a majority.

*   *   *

. . . So there it is. The decisions of the Supreme Court have had more effect on the reputation of the Court than the activities of its antagonists. The attitudes of the majority are favorable to the Court. In this informational environment, such decisions as the Court has been making (or at least the majority of those few decisions which rise to the public's threshold of awareness) are likely to be favorably communicated. To the extent that we can generalize from this study, we can expect a continuing consensus which is supportive of the Court.

This leaves us with two questions. One is the degree to which this Seattle study is an accurate indicator of the national pattern of attitudes toward the Court. Will the national pattern prove to be relatively homogeneous? Or will it prove to be heterogeneous with islands of support in certain parts of the country and centers of opposition located elsewhere? This is most important, and it is clear that we need a good national study of attitudes about the Court as soon as possible.

The other question is whether the joint effect of attitudes and communication here noted will prove to be general. If so, it could offer an explanation of why majorities and minorities on many political issues tend to persist for such long periods of time. Given these kinds of psychological roots, some dramatic new personality or issue or the addition of some new group of citizens is necessary to produce realignment. There are many cases in which realignment is not necessarily desirable. Support for the Supreme Court, for example, provides one anchor for our constitutional system. But if a conscientious minority cannot work in the arena of public opinion with reasonable hope of success, then we must provide them with some alternative way to give vent to their feelings. Otherwise their prospect is one of frustration, which in turn may lead to an embittered isolation or to an eventual explosion. Their feelings are going to find an outlet somewhere, and it is preferable that this expression be legitimate.

KENNETH DOLBEARE

The Supreme Court and the States: From Abstract Doctrine to Local Behavioral Conformity

* * *

Daniel Elazar has suggested a comparative political culture approach to the political behavior of American states and regions.[1] Differences in the political behavior of particular states *as states* have long been observed, of course, and what is distinctive about Elazar's work is mainly the effort to relate the causes, character, and results of these differences to his concept of political culture.[2] In developing his argument, he stresses the existence of distinct but patterned value premises, styles, concerns, and policy products in the politics of various states. The idea is plausible and provocative. Each political culture presumably would be distinctive also in terms of expectations toward courts, the legitimacy of various actions on the part of courts, and the general role of courts and the law within the polity. Such expectations, values, and experience would then also be major factors in shaping responses to Supreme Court decisions within a state.

1. Daniel Elazar, *American Federalism: A View From the States* (New York: Thomas Y. Crowell Co., 1966). See esp. Chs. 4 and 5, pp. 79–140. In speaking of the implementation of constitutional doctrines, he argues: "Although the national constitution may set the standard and the Supreme Court the guidelines, the state governments are left to apply those guidelines within their own boundaries in a manner consonant with their respective political cultures" (p. 7).

2. *Ibid.* Elazar offers no measures and no empirical support for his characterizations, relying chiefly on migration patterns developing out of original settlement differences.

From an unpublished essay by Mr. Dolbeare. Printed by permission.

Kenneth Dolbeare is Associate Professor of Political Science at the University of Wisconsin.

We can hardly expect to assess the relevance of these several dimensions of state political cultures without large-scale attitudinal and behavioral studies. Two primary indicators of the existence and importance of different political cultures may be explored briefly, however, as a means of supporting the utility of this approach. One factor affecting behavioral response to Supreme Court initiatives would be the set of attitudes and expectations which the affected, attentive, and general publics within the states hold toward the Supreme Court and the lower courts as institutions. Another would be the propensity of the people of the state to invoke the processes of courts and law for affecting the behavior of others. In both cases, we shall have to be content with inquiry limited to one or two dimensions of the subject. But the data which are developed in each strongly imply important effects from these aspects of state political culture.

Several recent studies provide some elements of background on public attitudes toward the Supreme Court and lower courts and judges.[3] Public orientations toward courts apparently change slowly over time if at all, as decisions and popular policy preferences (and other factors) interact. At any given moment, however, there is a general level of approval toward the Supreme Court and a set of expectations toward courts in general which form part of the political culture of the state. Two questions immediately arise: do these ratings and expectations vary between states? Do they affect reactions to decisions? Affirmative answers are essential to our thesis.

3. See John H. Kessel, "Public Perceptions of the Supreme Court," *Midwest Journal of Political Science*, Vol. 10 (May, 1966), pp. 167–191 (two-stage probability sample of 356 adults in two state legislative districts of Seattle, Wash., conducted by student interviewers); Kenneth M. Dolbeare, "The Public Views the Supreme Court" in Herbert Jacob (ed.), *Law and Politics in the Federal Courts* (Boston: Little, Brown & Co., 1967) (clustered area probability sample of 627 adults in Wisconsin conducted by the Wisconsin Survey Research Laboratory; Carl D. McMurray and Malcolm B. Parsons, "Public Attitudes Toward the Representational Role of Legislators and Judges," *Midwest Journal of Political Science*, Vol. 9 (May, 1965), pp. 167–185 ("random" sample of 207 white adults in Cape Kennedy area conducted by the Institute of Social Research of Florida State University); Kenneth M. Dolbeare and Phillip E. Hammond, "The Political Party Basis of Attitudes Toward the Supreme Court," *Public Opinion Quarterly* Vol. 32 (Spring, 1968), pp. 16–30. (re-analysis of six national surveys, four conducted by American Institute of Public Opinion, one by Michigan Survey Research Center and one by University of California (Berkeley) Survey Research Center).

The data presented in Table 1 [4] suggest that the answer to the first question is indeed affirmative. Not only do the states involved differ in attitudes toward the Court, but they vary in the extent to which political party identification correlates with ratings of the Court. Other research has indicated that party identification may be the primary cue for attitudes toward the Court; [5] if party plays a different structuring role in different states, there may be several dimensions of linkage to the basic political cultures of those states. There are serious problems of comparability encountered in any present attempt to find data bearing on these questions, and Table 1 has circumvented only some of them. But we may at least aver, in appropriately tentative terms, that there is support for this part of our thesis in what data can be developed short of a major new inquiry.

These findings might have been anticipated; perhaps even more readily predictable are differences between states in attitudes toward particular decisions. Table 2 contrasts responses to the most nearly comparable questions which could be found concerning the recent prayer decisions. The states in this instance were Minnesota and Texas, and they show sharp variation in reactions to the decisions involved. More revealing is the fact that here the variations showed *no* correlation with party identification, or, for that matter, with any other [6] demographic characteristic; other factors in the general political or religious experience of these states will obviously have to be considered in developing a general theory.

The available evidence also suggests an affirmative answer to the second question. Data from Minnesota show dramatically how the action of the Supreme Court may affect policy positions. Respondents in Minnesota were asked *first* whether they favored or opposed prayer at the start of the school day, and after their answers had been recorded, *then* were told that the Supreme Court had ruled the practice illegal and asked whether they liked the decision or not. Table 3

4. Data from the Texas and Minnesota Polls were made available through the courtesy of the Roper Center in Williamstown, Mass. The Berkeley data were specially prepared and made available by the University of California, Berkeley, Survey Research Center, by Mr. Stephen Steinberg, whose assistance was particularly helpful. The Wisconsin data were collected through the facilities of the Wisconsin Survey Research Laboratory, Harry Sharp, director. The assistance of all of these sources is gratefully acknowledged.
5. Dolbeare and Hammond, *op. cit.*
6. The Texas Poll, unfortunately, does not record religion of respondents.

Table 1

"RATINGS" OF U.S. SUPREME COURT

(A) Rating of Job Court is Doing

	Wisconsin,[1] 1966	Seattle, Wash.,[2] 1965	Texas,[3] 1964
Very Good/Good	62%	51%	46%
Fair/Poor	38%	49%	54%
	100%	100%	100%
	N = 625	N = 323	N = 1000

(B) Rating of Job Court is Doing, By Political Party

	United States,[4] 1964		Wisconsin,[1] 1966		Seattle, Wash.,[2] 1965		Texas,[3] 1964	
	Dem	Rep	Dem	Rep	Dem	Rep	Dem	Rep
Very Good/Good	65%	51%	71%	55%	61%	37%	51%	44%
Fair/Poor	35%	49%	29%	45%	39%	63%	49%	56%
	100%	100%	100%	100%	100%	100%	100%	100%
	N = 1314	N = 1052	N = 191	N = 147	N = 152	N = 134	N = 558	N = 77

1. Wisconsin Survey, 1966. Q. How good a job do you feel the U.S. Supreme Court has been doing lately? (Very Good/Good/Fair/Poor/Don't Know). "Don't Know" responses (19% of total) eliminated.
2. See John Kessel, "Public Perceptions of the Supreme Court," *Midwest Journal of Political Science*, Vol. 10 (May 1966) p. 179. Q. Speaking generally, how would you describe your own feelings about the Supreme Court? (Coded into Strong Supporter/Supporter/Neutral/Critic, which have been equated here with Very Good/Good/Fair/Poor for comparative purposes. Nonresponses unspecified, but other indications suggest 10% of total.)
3. Texas Poll, 1964. Q. In general, what kind of rating would you give the U.S. Supreme Court—excellent, good, fair or poor? (Excellent/Good/Fair/Poor/No opinion). "No opinion" responses (15% of total) eliminated. Q. The Supreme Court is doing a good job these days.· (All agreement responses included under Very Good/Good; all disagreement included under Fair/Poor.
4. Berkeley Survey Research Center, 1964. South eliminated. Q. The Supreme Court is doing a good job these days.· (All agreement responses included under Very Good/Good; all disagreement included under Fair/Poor. Noncomparability acknowledged, data included as the only available national standard.)

Table 2

APPROVAL AND DISAPPROVAL OF SUPREME COURT DECISIONS [1]
IN MINNESOTA AND TEXAS

(A) *Approval/Disapproval of Prayer/Bible Reading Decisions*

	Approval	Disapproval	Don't Know, Don't Care	
Minnesota,[2] 1962	55%	31%	14%	100% (N = 586)
Texas,[3]	28%	60%	12%	100% (N = 1000)

(B) *Approval/Disapproval of Prayer/Bible Reading Decisions, By Political Party*

	Minnesota, 1962		Texas, 1964	
Response to decisions preventing prayers/ Bible reading in schools	D-F-L	Rep	Dem	Rep
Approve	65	65	34	34
Disapprove	35	35	66	66
	100%	100%	100%	100%
	N = 223	N = 148	N = 599	N = 82

1. The decisions were different although related ones, of course: *Engel v. Vitale,* 370 U.S. 421 (1962) and *Abington Township v Schempp,* 374 U.S. 203 (1963). The differences in response are so substantial, however, that the comparison is worth making. Nor is "approval" of a decision necessarily indicative of anything respecting behavior. Opinion research by political scientists should take care to seek out the prospects of action rather than settling for this indeterminate commercial inquiry.

2. Q. The U.S. Supreme Court has ruled recently that it is not legal to have the school board or any public official or agency prepare one certain prayer for school children to recite in the public schools. Do you like the Supreme Court ruling? dislike it? or don't you care one way or the other? (Like it/Dislike it/ Don't care/No opinion/Other). Minnesota Poll No. 214, 1962.

3. Q. The U.S. Supreme Court has ruled that no state or local government may require the reading of the Lord's Prayer or Bible verses in public schools. What are your views on this? (Approve/Disapprove/Don't Know). Texas Poll, 1964.

shows how the Court's action blurred policy preference; nearly half of those favoring prayer nevertheless "liked" the decision! This effect may be partially attributable to general orientations toward government action, but the implication is strong that it is caused by some form of halo effect from the symbolic image of the Supreme Court.

Table 3

RESPONSE TO COURT DECISION BY PREFERENCE FOR PRAYER

Supreme Court has ruled against it— do you like it or dislike it? [2]	Should there be prayer in Minnesota schools? [1]	
	Favor (74%)	Oppose (26%)
like it	44%	89%
dislike it	44%	4%
don't care	12%	7%
	100%	100%
	N = 395	N = 135

Q. 1. In the public schools of some states, the school day is opened with a time for prayer by the children. Do you favor or oppose having a time for prayer as part of each school day in Minnesota's public schools? (Favor/ Oppose/No opinion/Other).

Q. 2. The U.S. Supreme Court has ruled recently that it is not legal to have the school board or any public official or agency prepare one certain prayer for school children to recite in the public schools. Do you like the Supreme Court ruling? dislike it? or don't you care one way or the other? (Like it/Dislike it/ Don't care/No opinion/Other). (Asked immediately after question 1 above.)

We know from the Wisconsin study that persons subscribing to the "myths" of nonpartisan, mechanical jurisprudence are more likely to rate the Court highly than are persons who see the Justices as exercising discretionary, policymaking functions.[7] The extent to which such "myths" are held and the general prestige level of the Supreme Court vary between states; they are background elements of the political cultures of the states which combine with policy preferences and other values to establish the context in which Supreme Court initiatives are received.

*   *   *

The identification and exploration of the varying levels of expectations toward courts which are embedded in the political cultures of the states should be followed by documentation of the relevance of such attitudes to behavior. At present, we have only the hint that propensity to act in opposition to a Supreme Court decision is more

7. Dolbeare, op. cit. note 3 above.

a function of a sense of political efficacy than of one's generally unfavorable view of the Court.[8] It seems likely that further research
would show more direct impact of attitudes on behavior, and that
general expectations toward courts have an important structuring
effect on local responses to Supreme Court policy pronouncements.

The second aspect of state political culture previously projected as
relevant to local responses to Supreme Court decisions was the propensity of political actors to employ the law and the courts to gain
their ends. Decisions of the Supreme Court are only rarely self-
executing, and for the most part they must be asserted by litigants in
various ways before they begin to have widespread behavioral impact.
The litigiousness of a state's population then may bear upon the
process of conversion of doctrine into practice; do the states differ in
this respect?

Again, the evidence indicates that they do. . . .

*   *   *

Intrastate diversities make any characterization of the political
culture of "a state" a somewhat tentative enterprise, and there are
additional problems here in the development of empirical measures.
Use of court workload data as a means of assessing litigiousness,
though attractive and practical,[9] is not satisfactory without controlling
for important intervening factors; the workloads of state courts of last
resort are variably affected by the courts' jurisdictional discretion,
and trial court workload may be affected by the availability of
lawyers, the financial capacity of litigants, or other extraneous factors.

*   *   *

. . . Such higher incidence of use of courts is significant in itself,
but it may also suggest further possibilities, such as preference for
courts over open political processes, greater finality for the decisions

8. Dolbeare, *op. cit.* note 3 above.
9. The Council of State Governments, in a series of publications, has provided a potentially valuable source of comparative state data. See, e.g., *Workloads of State Courts of Last Resort* (Chicago: Council of State Governments,
1962).

of courts or a greater role for "legal" rather than "practical" solutions to problems.

These two characteristics of the political cultures of states—images and expectations toward courts, and litigiousness—are by no means a comprehensive catalogue of the court-related aspects of state political cultures. Nor would such factors be the only ones relevant to setting the context of response to Supreme Court doctrine within the states. But they do indicate that such factors are integral to general theories of behavioral response to Supreme Court acts involving social change.